POWER

HOW TO BE SPIRITUALLY BUFF

RON SHIPLEY

UP

POWER

HOW TO BE SPIRITUALLY BUFF

RON SHIPLEY

UP

REDEMPTION PRESS

Published by Redemption Press, PO Box 427, Enumclaw, WA 98022.

Toll-Free (844) 2REDEEM (273-3336)

Redemption Press is honored to present this title in partnership with the author. The views expressed or implied in this work are those of the author. Redemption Press provides our imprint seal representing design excellence, creative content, and high-quality production.

ISBN 13: 978-1-64645-021-3 (Paperback)
　　　　 978-1-64645-022-0 (ePub)
　　　　 978-1-64645-023-7 (Mobi)

Library of Congress Catalog Card Number: 2020903675

CONTENTS

PREFACE

ALMOST THIRTY-SIX YEARS AGO, I was about to finish up at Grace Seminary. I had been in the Air Force for almost ten years before attending Grace, so I was a little older than most of my fellow students. During my last semester there, some of my professors asked me, "Since you're older than most of your fellow students, what do you think we could have taught you more about?" It didn't take much thinking on my part to give them my answer. I responded, "I know so little about the Holy Spirit." One of the professors smiled and said, "You're absolutely right, and once you have time to study on the subject, you need to write a book about Him."

Well, here I am, retired after thirty years in the pastorate and still burdened about the church's lack of understanding concerning the third person of the Godhead. No, I still don't have all the answers, but He has been so empowering to me over the years. I believe that most Christians are quenching and grieving Him every day simply because they don't know Him the way they should.

I pray that the pages that follow will enlighten you in your relationship with the Holy Spirit and will enhance your walk of faith. God the Father, Jesus Christ the Son, and the Holy Spirit—who is the Comforter and much more—are the Three in One, and they equally desire to have a relationship with you and me so we can be the called ones they have made us to be.

Verses you have memorized or meditated on are about to come alive for you. The spiritual battle is also going to become more intensified for you. Once you see how you fit into the big picture, you will see what an important part you have to play in the body of Christ. Just remember—you are more than a conqueror, and you already have the victory.

It is time the Enemy appreciates you for who you really are: a soldier of the cross who is unwilling to give any more ground to the one who is already defeated.

As we begin this adventure, I believe it will change your life. As your life is transformed, the lives of many others will also be changed as you allow the Spirit to take control and empower you.

INTRODUCTION

DO YOU KNOW HOW many people don't read the preface or introduction of a book? I don't know what the percentage is, but I have found over the years, in speaking with countless pastors and fellow Christians, it appears to be high. What's more important right here and right now is that you are reading this one. That tells me you have a willing spirit to learn. That is why I am writing this book on the Holy Spirit—that you might learn the truth about Him and truly be changed. As you go through the pages of this book, please know that my intent is to teach you. I want you to know I will be there with you, sentence by sentence, praying that you are captured by the truths of God's Word.

The whole doctrine of the Holy Spirit has been derailed. This has happened through Satan's deception and humanity's old nature responding through emotions instead of following scriptural truth.

One of the great practical truths I learned while in seminary was that when a Christian experiences something different than what is presented in the Word as doctrine, he or she will almost always go with the experience instead of the doctrine. When this takes place, it will invariably result in confusion within the body of Christ. Because of this, the Spirit's ministry within the church of Jesus Christ is but a shadow of the powerful reality He is supposed to have.

The intent of each chapter in this book is to establish a solid foundation of who the Spirit is, what He is to the individual believer, and what He desires to do as your Comforter.

The Holy Spirit's ministry is to help us become like our Lord and Savior, Jesus Christ. This is why Jesus told His disciples that He was going to the Father and was going to ask Him to send "another" (in the Greek, this is "one just like me"), so the One who was coming was going to be the third person of the Godhead—the Holy Spirit (John 14:16).

Join me and see the great practical truths about the One who wants to empower you to become the extraordinary person God intends you to be.

As John declares in his gospel, "But the Advocate, the Holy Spirit, whom the Father will send in my name, will teach you all things" (John 14:26). So prepare for some of the greatest spiritual insights the Bible has to offer you. Then it is up to you to live your life as more than a conqueror, empowered and led by the Holy Spirit.

I look back over my life and see how the Lord has used me over and over again in my second career as a janitor. To most people, this would seem like a ho-hum job, but for me it has been a privilege to share the Lord and minister in a non-church setting. I have approached both my pastoral work and my janitorial work as opportunities to bring glory to my Lord. When you do this, no matter what your job, you will have divine appointments along the way.

Whatever it is that you are doing—no matter how long you have been doing it—are you doing it to bring glory to the Lord? Life can be very rewarding if we make ourselves available to the Holy Spirit's leading. Be ready for what He has in store for you, especially in those everyday, ordinary situations.

Faith is to be the means by which Christians do what they do. "Whatever you do, work at it with all your heart, as working for the Lord, not for human masters" (Colossians 3:23). This is where our sensitivity to the Holy Spirit's leading, teaching, empowering, and more is essential. Otherwise we will miss some of the greatest opportunities we will ever have to be Christlike, no matter what we are doing.

So come alongside me during the time it takes to go on this journey, and please don't rush through it. Take the time so you can put it into practice for yourself. And if you don't know already, you will discover as we travel on that you have One who wants to teach and guide you in the truth.

Our time together is intended to get you to slow down and establish a richer relationship with the Holy Spirit. Let Him have His place in your life and begin to do for you what He has wanted to do since the very moment He sealed you at your salvation.

R. Shipley

Chapter 1

THE HOLY SPIRIT
IS A VERY REAL PERSON

*All this I have spoken while still with you. But
the Advocate, the Holy Spirit, whom the Father
will send in my name, will teach you all things
and will remind you of everything I have said
to you.*
John 14:25–26

TOO MANY CHRISTIANS REFER to the Holy
Spirit as "It." Because of this, many people miss
the reality that the Holy Spirit is the third person of the
Godhead—with whom we are to have a relationship.

My primary goal in writing this book is that you
might realize that the Holy Spirit is there for each
believer—for you—to know personally. Once you enter

this relationship and understand the part that you have, your perspective of the spiritual world will become much more real and exciting.

My intent in this first chapter is to establish the foundational truth that the Holy Spirit is a person who wants to work in and through your life so you can accomplish the will of God.

Yes, the Holy Spirit is a person. He is divine, but is still an individual who has special ministries to every believer. As a person, He can be ignored, neglected, quenched, and even grieved. (All these describe actions that are taken against a person.)

There is a wealth of information about the person who is revealed to us as the Holy Spirit. In the New Testament alone, there are over two hundred individual references to Him and His ministry to Jesus, believers, the church, and even the unbelieving world. The question is, will you take these truths and personalize your relationship with Him, allowing Him to have that place in your life He has wanted since the day He sealed you?

You may be saying to yourself, *Well, of course He is a person.* Yet so few Christians actually treat Him as one. In my early years of adulthood, I can remember hearing again and again, (in several different fundamental churches) the Spirit of God, mentioned in the Old Testament, was just the power of God going into the world to have an impact. He was presented as nothing more than the means by which the Father accomplishes His goals.

Let's begin our journey by looking at His equality with the Father and Son.

Fact 1: He Was There before the Beginning

> Then God said, "Let us make mankind in our image, in our likeness." (Genesis 1:26)

Here we see the Hebrew word *Elohim*, the three-in-one Godhead. This word is pronounced "el-ō-hēm." This word is used to confirm that the third person was there in the Godhead, not just as a source of power, but as a member of the Trinity. Together they determined to create human beings in their image and likeness.

What has happened? How have we gotten to where most believers treat the Spirit as if He doesn't exist or is of little importance? Join me, and it will become clear how we arrived at this place and how we can break through the barriers to have a vibrant relationship with Him.

Possibly the greatest sin in our lives is when we personally grieve and even quench the Holy Spirit's influence upon us. Are "grieving the Holy Spirit" and "quenching the Holy Spirit" just figures of speech, or are they real, personal reactions on the part of the Holy Spirit to you and me sinning?

Before we consider other equally important passages, come with me to the gospel of John. When I read John's gospel, I am taken back to the many times I heard fellow pastors remark that there is little said to us in the Bible about the Holy Spirit. This further emphasizes how deeply Satan's deception has affected the church, the body of Jesus Christ.

Listen closely to the very words of our Lord Himself with regard to the third person of the Godhead.

Fact 2: He's the Sent One

> And I will ask the Father, and he will give you another advocate to help you and be with you forever—the Spirit of truth. The world cannot accept him, because it neither sees him nor knows him. But you know him, for he lives with you and will be in you. I will not leave you as orphans; I will come to you. Before long, the world will not see me anymore, but you will see me. Because I live, you also will live. On that day you will realize that I am in my Father, and you are in me, and I am in you. Whoever has my commands and keeps them is the one who loves me. The one who loves me will be loved by my Father, and I too will love them and show myself to them. (John 14:16–21)

Is Jesus speaking here of a person or just about some power or force? You may think I am being repetitive here, but I ask this because, for all practical purposes, He is being ignored as a real person in the individual believer's life. What about you? Do you, right now, have a growing relationship with Him? Look at just some of His ministries for you:

- Is He your Comforter?
- Is He leading you?
- Has He filled you?
- Has He empowered you?
- Is He teaching you?

I could go on—and I will later—but this should be enough for you to begin to personally evaluate your own relationship with the Holy Spirit. We will now move on to those other important passages.

> All this I have spoken while still with you. But the Advocate, the Holy Spirit, whom the Father will send in my name, will teach you all things and will remind you of everything I have said to you. (John 14:25–26)

This One, whom Jesus asked the Father to send and then was sent, wants to teach us all things and bring all things to our minds. The Advocate, or Comforter, is one who draws alongside, not to be a silent partner, but to personally minister to us.

Jesus knew His disciples would need all the help they could get, so here He promised to send the Helper. The Holy Spirit wasn't sent just to the disciples, but to every believer.

Will we take this to heart and allow the Holy Spirit to do what He was sent to do? You'll see as we proceed that these verses are all foundational truths that declare that if we are not daily interacting with the Holy Spirit as our Comforter, we are purposefully sinning against the third person of the Godhead—and therefore are opposing the will of God.

Next, look at how Jesus takes us another step into our need to have a biblical relationship with the Spirit:

> When the Advocate comes, whom I will send to you from the Father—the Spirit of truth

> who goes out from the Father—he will testify
> about me. And you also must testify, for you
> have been with me from the beginning. (John
> 15:26–27)

This One is the Spirit of truth, and the main theme of His ministry is Jesus Christ—the very One you and I are supposed to be becoming more like every day of our lives. As a result of His ministry in our lives, we then can declare the truth about the Son of God. (I know this passage is specifically directed at His original disciples, but as we read in the apostle Paul's epistles, it becomes obvious the instruction is also to us.)

Then Jesus adds still another part of the Holy Spirit's doctrine:

> But very truly I tell you, it is for your good
> that I am going away. Unless I go away, the
> Advocate will not come to you; but if I go, I
> will send him to you. When he comes, he will
> prove the world to be in the wrong about sin
> and righteousness and judgment: about sin,
> because people do not believe in me; about
> righteousness, because I am going to the
> Father, where you can see me no longer; and
> about judgment, because the prince of this
> world now stands condemned.
>
> I have much more to say to you, more than
> you can now bear. But when he, the Spirit of
> truth, comes, he will guide you into all the
> truth. He will not speak on his own; he will
> speak only what he hears, and he will tell you
> what is yet to come. He will glorify me because
> it is from me that he will receive what he will

make known to you. All that belongs to the Father is mine. That is why I said the Spirit will receive from me what he will make known to you. (John 16:7–15)

What tremendous truths about the Spirit are laid down here before us!

- He was sent by Christ to convict the world of sin, righteousness, and judgment.
- He will guide us into all truth.
- He will speak what the Father and Son tell Him.
- He will reveal what is coming.
- He will glorify Christ.
- He will reveal everything of the Godhead that needs to be revealed.

With all of this in mind, I ask you: Are you listening to Him?

Now let me help you digest what John 14–16 says about the Spirit:

- He is the Helper, but for Him to help you, you must have a relationship with Him. Otherwise, as things take place in your life, you'll downgrade them to just circumstances rather than evidence of the Spirit's work and an opportunity to seek His help. Remember, for someone to be able to help you, you must desire and accept their help.
- He is to be your Teacher. I must first be a listener before I can be taught. Are you listening for His teachings? Of course, the source of His teaching is the Scriptures, so are you in the Word faithfully?

- He will help us remember. I have heard people say, "No matter how much effort I put in, I just can't remember what I have studied." There are many possible reasons for this. Not listening, having quenched or grieved Him, not being filled with Him, not being empowered by Him, and walking on our own, are just a few examples.

Fact 3: You and I Can Directly Impact Him

> And do not grieve the Holy Spirit of God, with whom you were sealed for the day of redemption. (Ephesians 4:30)

Don't bring sorrow to the One who has sealed you. This means that the moment you were saved, the Holy Spirit placed a spiritual seal upon you, so that you cannot lose your salvation.

Don't grieve Him. Just in case you don't think this is saying what it appears to be saying, listen: the Greek word for "grieve" literally means "to distress, to make sad, and to bring heaviness to." These are things you can only do to a person, not to a force or power.

I remember times as a pastor when I heard parents trying to teach their teenagers about responsibility at a job. I heard some of the best instruction that could be given, and then I watched the teens totally ignore their parents' advice. At those times, I witnessed great heartache on the part of parents. Now just think about us doing this same thing to the One who wants to personally minister to us. The Holy Spirit wants to give us input and wisdom for our lives, yet we often ignore Him. Give the Holy Spirit His full place in your life and be blessed.

Look what else we must avoid:

> Quench not the Spirit. (1 Thessalonians 5:19
> KJV)

The primary meaning of this word "quench" is "to extinguish." Think of it—just as you can put out a fire by quenching it with water, you can do the same to the Holy Spirit's desired power and influence upon your life. We can never forget that He was sent by the Father to have a direct, powerful influence on you and me.

For instance, when you read the Bible, do you just engage your brain with the words, or do you begin by asking the Holy Spirit to teach you? When you minister to another person, do you ask the Holy Spirit for guidance about how best to minister? He is always there, but if we live our lives through our own head knowledge and don't allow Him to lead us, we are quenching His influence upon our lives.

It is important to bring up another passage that uses this same word since we will be dealing with our Enemy in chapter 2. Don't miss the contrast; it is astounding.

> Take up the shield of faith, with which you
> can extinguish all the flaming arrows of the
> evil one. (Ephesians 6:16)

Isn't it amazing that as believers we can have two extraordinary influences? We can quench the Holy Spirit's power in our lives, and we can quench all the fiery darts of our greatest enemy, Satan. If those are not two extremes that directly influence our lives, I don't know what is. With either of these truths, we can have head knowledge about it and yet never do the right thing.

We can be visibly moved by a truth and yet never put it into practice. So often in my own life, I've found myself engaging just my head knowledge rather than living out the practical wisdom the Holy Spirit has revealed to me. Don't ever forget that what we are looking at is a growth process. As we utilize what He shows us, we are changed, and it becomes more natural to us.

Knowing these truths and yet not making practical application of them is like having the most powerful car on the road, but never putting the key in and turning it on. What a waste! Yet so many Christians are going through their everyday lives powerless because they have not yet surrendered to the person of the Holy Spirit and allowed Him to take the lead.

Fact 4: He Inspired the Truth of God's Word

Don't miss this tremendous truth that Peter reveals to us:

> Prophecy never had its origin in the human will, but prophets, though human, spoke from God as they were carried along by the Holy Spirit. (2 Peter 1:21)

There He was—moving the writers of Scripture to write what the Godhead wanted written. It was not some mere force or influence, but it was the third person of the Godhead moving them in a very personal way. He wants to continue to move you and me in this same personal way—not through writing Scripture, but through living the truth of the Scriptures, so we can directly impact the world around us for eternity.

With each of the following chapters, I am praying that you, if it is not already true for you, will be brought to a place of humbly surrendering to the will of the Holy Spirit and becoming all that God the Father, the Son, and the Holy Spirit intend for you to be.

Prayer of Confession and Hope

> *Blessed Spirit*, thank You for all You have done in my life. Please forgive me for those times I have grieved You, quenched You, and just neglected You for who You are. I love You. Please empower me by filling me with Your presence as I give up more and more of myself and allow You to take charge of my life. Amen.

Chapter 2

THE FALLEN ONE

I **HAD ONLY BEEN IN** the ministry for seven years when I received word that my dad was very ill and was in the hospital. I had been witnessing to him for years about being saved, but he never responded. In fact, things had gotten so bad that my mother asked my wife and me to stop talking to him about the Bible. So when I received word of his hospitalization, I drove by myself three hours from northwestern Ohio to northwestern Indiana to spend time with him. But before I left, I called five pastor friends and asked them to be praying for me. Little did I know what lay ahead.

When I got to the hospital, Dad was very weak but quite alert. I helped him sit up on the side of the bed.

When I began sharing Christ with him, a startling spiritual battle began to be waged against me. The young man in the bed next to Dad sat up and began using some of the most profane words I had ever heard. He did everything but growl at me. I laid my dad back down in his bed and went over to the young man. I pointed my finger right at him and said, "If my dad dies right now, he will step into the fires of hell for eternity. What about you?"

What happened next still sends chills up my back. The young man laid back down, pulled the covers up to his chin, closed his eyes, and pretended to go to sleep. I felt very empowered as I went back to my dad, helped him sit back up, and continued talking to him about his need for Christ. The only difference now was that I spoke even louder. Then it happened: Dad asked Jesus to forgive him and to become his Savior! Then a huge smile spread across my dad's face like I had never seen before.

I thank God to this day that I contacted my friends to pray for me, because I could tell them how they were part of the spiritual victory in that hospital room that night. My dad lived for seven more days, and then—praise God—he went home to the Lord.

That, my friends, was just one of the many experiences I have had in quenching the fiery darts of Satan. All this took place because the Holy Spirit moved me to contact my friends before I went to see my dad. You will see later that praying for one another is an important part of putting on and using the armor of God.

Lucifer has become Satan, the fallen angel, the god of

this world, the prince of the power of the air, the adversary, the devil, the tempter, Beelzebul, the wicked one, the ruler of this world, Belial, and the accuser of our brethren. He goes by many different names and titles, and he also utilizes many different approaches in trying to deceive and malign the body of Jesus Christ. The Bible refers to these approaches as "wiles," "fiery darts," and "schemes" (Ephesians 6:11, 16). These fiery darts can be very hot and very penetrating.

As we begin this chapter, here is one of the most revealing passages in all the Word:

> For the mystery of lawlessness doth already work: only there is one that restraineth now, until he be taken out of the way. (2 Thessalonians 2:7 ASV)

There is so much that comes into play in the above truth, some of which we will look at in chapter 5. For this chapter, though, let me just say that the ones who are capitalizing on the lawlessness, or sin, are Satan, his spiritual minions, and his human followers.

A lot has been written about Satan. Let's allow the Holy Spirit, through the apostle Paul, to expose one of the most important truths:

> Finally, be strong in the Lord and in his mighty power. Put on the full armor of God, so that you can take your stand against the devil's schemes. For our struggle is not against flesh and blood, but against the rulers, against the authorities, against the powers of this dark

world and against the spiritual forces of evil in
the heavenly realms. (Ephesians 6:10–12)

In leadership over all the above spiritual beings is
none other than Satan himself. These wicked dignitaries
are those angels who follow Satan as he wars against God
and the people of God.

Now that we have seen (in chapter 1) that the Word
of God has established that the Holy Spirit is a person, I
want to draw your attention to the one who has been at
the center of the deception that has made many Christians ignorant of the person of the Holy Spirit and His
desired work in our lives.

I am convinced that Satan's most influential fiery
dart has been to depersonalize the third person of the
Godhead—and he has done an exceptional job. While
I was in the military, I heard time and again, "You must
know your enemy." Following this line of thought, we
must first focus on his character. Please consider this
passage of truth that comes right from the lips of Jesus:

> You belong to your father, the devil, and you
> want to carry out your father's desires. He was
> a murderer from the beginning, not holding to
> the truth, for there is no truth in him. When
> he lies, he speaks his native language, for he is
> a liar and the father of lies. (John 8:44)

I believe that at the heart of Satan's deception was
the creation of the caricature of the little guy in the
red suit with the pitchfork. As a result, humankind in
general (including even many religious people) has all

but fictionalized him. To them he is not any more real than the Easter Bunny or Father Time. My intent in this chapter is to bring him out of the shadows of deception and make it very clear who he is and what he utilizes to disable the body of Jesus Christ—and in particular, you and me. His attacks are double-pronged: he attacks from without (our adversary) and from within (our tempter).

In the following verse, observe the work of this one who is pure evil, for it reveals the influence he has had, even upon some of the angels in glory:

> His tail drew the third part of the stars of heaven, and did cast them to the earth: and the dragon stood before the woman which was ready to be delivered, for to devour her child as soon as it was born. (Revelation 12:4 KJV)

This verse has been interpreted in many different ways, so let me just draw from it the basic truths. At some point Satan left heaven, but he is still able to return to rail against believers. Further, he has a following of demons here and now. There is much more in this text, but suffice it to say that he is here, and he has a following.

Throughout the Old Testament, we discover how the devil tried time and again to destroy the messianic line, so Jesus could not come into the world. The first note of this enemy of Christ in the Bible is found in Genesis 3:14–15 (NKJV):

> So the LORD God said to the serpent: "Because you have done this, you are cursed more than all cattle, and more than every beast of the

field; on your belly you shall go, and you shall eat dust all the days of your life. And I will put enmity between you and the woman, and between your seed and her Seed; He shall bruise your head, and you shall bruise His heel."

The first half of this passage is obviously directed toward the snake, but the second part is directed toward Satan for having used the creature to bring about the temptation. As the story of Scripture moves forward, this prediction plays itself out.

These actions of the devil throughout the Old Testament clearly reveal his depraved, empty heart. But before his fall, there he was in glory—a perfectly created being made to serve the God of all creation. Yet after his fall, being held in the claws of his own pride, we see him trying to disrupt God's sovereign plan.

This is why I have this chapter in my book about the Holy Spirit. As essential as it is that we develop a relationship with the person of the Holy Spirit, we must also know our Enemy as revealed in the Bible, so we can successfully fight the good fight. We don't want to quench the Holy Spirit in our lives, but we must purpose to quench the fiery darts of the wicked one. This will become more practical when we get into chapter 5, "The Priceless Armor of God."

Now back to our brief examination of Satan's attempts to break the messianic lineage. For example, we see his attempt to cause King David to number the people (1 Chronicles 21:1). You may be asking, "But how does this action play into Satan's plan to keep the Messiah from coming?" King David was in the direct lineage of the Messiah. By getting David to number the people (an act of pride), the devil may have hoped that God would take David's life and thus directly affect the lineage. Remember, unlike God, Satan is just a created being—powerful, but still a created being. His plans and knowledge are always limited by his finiteness.

In chapters 1–2 of the book of Job, we are given tremendous insight into the person of Satan and his attacking of humankind (as God allows him). But we are also given a clear presentation of Satan's limitation before Almighty God. Please take the time to read it for yourself and see the complete control your Father has over your Enemy. Don't be quick to say, "But that was Job." Yes, and if you know the Lord as your personal Savior, you, too, are most precious to the Almighty, and therefore you are a target of Satan. In fact, as you will see in chapter 6, you are now the temple of the living God, because the Holy Spirit came to live in you when He sealed you at your salvation.

Let's consider just one more Old Testament passage:

> And he shewed me Joshua the high priest standing before the angel of the LORD, and Satan standing at his right hand to resist him. (Zechariah 3:1 KJV)

We have established by Old Testament Scripture that there is indeed a created individual who has power to impact people as God allows. When we transition into the New Testament, we observe how Satan continues on his mission to keep the Messiah from His mission. Not being able to stop the coming of the Lord during his Old Testament attempts, Satan's next move was to tempt the heart of an evil king (Herod) to kill the child after His birth (Matthew 2:16).

Granted, we are not told specifically that Satan tempted or directed Herod to take these actions, but the darkness that was in Herod's heart to kill all those babies came directly from the iniquity that was and is at work in our world. And who is in the lead in this evil world? "The god of this age" (2 Corinthians 4:4). To this I want to add another most revealing and powerful passage of Scripture: "The thief [Satan] comes only to steal and kill" (John 10:10).

It is most interesting to me to see Satan's attempts to orchestrate everyday life situations to gain his ends. Of course, the more he goes unnoticed, the more he can accomplish his goals. So again, we must know our Enemy!

After not being able to gain his goal through Herod, he later directly tempted Jesus three times in the wilderness (Matthew 4:1–11). But Christ, being the Son of the living God and faithful to His Father's will, took the Word of God and quoted it back to Satan, powerfully thwarting his attempts. This, my friend, is utilizing the sword of the Spirit, which is a piece of the spiritual armor God gives us to fight our spiritual battles.

We again see Satan's arrogance, even before Christ. Luke's account says that after Satan tempted Jesus, he left Jesus "for a season" (Luke 4:13 KJV). Satan doesn't give up. He is on a mission, and you and I are now his targets. He hunts like "a roaring lion . . . seeking whom he may devour" (1 Peter 5:8 KJV). But please don't panic. Take to heart the following truth: "In all these things we are more than conquerors through him who loved us" (Romans 8:37).

I can hardly wait for you to get to chapter 5, where I will share with you the amazing spiritual armor that has been given to us to use daily. But before we do that, I want to help us keep a good balance in our spiritual walk. Look at what the apostle John declares in his first letter: "The whole world is under the control of the evil one" (1 John 5:19).

This is one of the main reasons Jesus asked the Father to send the Comforter (Holy Spirit) to do His special work in our lives (John 14:16–31). We must depend upon His spiritual help to be able to win our daily battles and to grow spiritually.

You might be thinking, *Does the Trinity have to adjust to Satan's powers?* Far from it! The statement in 1 John 5 is all part of your heavenly Father's plans. The word "under" in verse 19 means "to be appointed." While we know we are God's, the world right now is appointed to be under the power of Satan. But wait! Why would God allow such a thing? Because sin deserves punishment and judgment, and the fallen world still lies in darkness until Christ comes again. With the Holy Spirit working in and through our lives, we become more like Christ. We can then impact the world for Him, and the iniquity is further restrained—for now.

Look at one more declaration about Satan's character,

this time from Jesus Himself. We must never forget that the Lord knew Satan from the moment He had created him. Listen closely to these revealing words of Jesus as He challenged the people who were there with Him by telling them that if they loved Him, God would be their Father. What a change takes place when we become Christians! But look at the character of the one we are following before we are saved:

> You belong to your father, the devil, and you want to carry out your father's desires. He was a murderer from the beginning, not holding to the truth, for there is no truth in him. When he lies, he speaks his native language, for he is a liar and the father of lies. (John 8:44)

Why would Satan directly attack the doctrine of the person of the Holy Spirit? Just as he knows that Jesus is the Son of God, so too, he knows that the Holy Spirit is very God and is essential to each individual in the body of Christ.

As you'll see later, Satan regularly attacks different aspects of the Spirit's personal ministries to believers. Having known and dwelt in the presence of pure truth and righteousness, Satan has an ability to deceive and distort the truth about the Holy Spirit. We must know all we can about our Enemy and his schemes against the Holy Spirit. Our relationship with the Holy Spirit is our power, strength, comfort, and source of spiritual gifts and spiritual direction. Through this relationship, not only can we walk in faith, but we can also live a powerful, successful life of faith.

If in any way you still doubt that Satan can have an influence upon the Christian, listen to what Paul tells the believers of Thessalonica about Satan's direct influence upon him: "For we wanted to come to you—certainly I, Paul, did, again and again—but Satan blocked our way" (1 Thessalonians 2:18).

This was written by the apostle Paul, who had victory after victory over Satan and his demons. Please take it to heart: you and I need the Holy Spirit's power in our lives.

There's much more in the Bible about Satan. I hope you will research for yourself the titles and names I mentioned at the beginning of this chapter, being sure to look up each of the verses referenced. However, in the limited space of this book, I don't want to spend any more time dealing with our adversary.

Satan is your enemy, and the better you understand him and his ways, the better soldier you will be for the cross—and the more the Holy Spirit will be able to accomplish through your life, to further the kingdom of God in the here and now. This will become clearer to you as we consider the armor and our use of it against Satan and his attacks upon us.

Let me close out this chapter with one more look into the character of our enemy. Isaiah 14:12–15 was a historical declaration against an earthly king, but many scholars declare that it is also a look into the heart of hearts of none other than Lucifer himself. What we see is this one who started out in glory, but because of his prideful acts, he had the greatest fall of all of God's created beings.

> How you have fallen from heaven, morning star, son of the dawn! You have been cast down to the earth, you who once laid low the nations! You said in your heart, "I will ascend to the heavens; I will raise my throne above the stars of God; I will sit enthroned on the mount of assembly, on the utmost heights of Mount Zaphon. I will ascend above the tops of the clouds; I will make myself like the Most High." But you are brought down to the realm of the dead, to the depths of the pit. (Isaiah 14:12–15)

Please take the time to digest this passage of Scripture. If you do, I am convinced you will receive the greatest look into the heart of the Enemy. Pride was the source of his spiritual/physical fall, and pride is what still blinds him and motivates him today.

A Side Note

As I have said before and will say again, this book is intended to be an introduction to your personal relationship with the Holy Spirit. I don't want to muddy the waters, but I think it is important to try to assist in any way I can.

Theologians are not all in agreement in their interpretation of the above area of Scripture, but even if these passages are not directly speaking of Satan, they summarize well what caused his fall from grace.

The only place in the King James Bible where you find the name Lucifer is in Isaiah 14:12. I believe this was

Satan's original name before he fell from glory. As you see in the text, this name means "son of the morning" or "morning star." As you proceed through the rest of Isaiah 14 and also consider Ezekiel 28:11–19, you see the condemnation of a powerful earthly leader—but woven in and through the text is also the Lord's condemnation of a special heavenly being, and Satan is the only one who fits the blame.

I include this to remind us that when we make life all about us, we are as far as we can get from where God wants us to be. Our duty is to faithfully follow Jesus in His humility and submission to the Father's will, and the only way we can do this is by following the lead of the Holy Spirit.

Prayer for Clarity

> *Lord Jesus*, please help me to humble myself under the Holy Spirit's control and to gain the wisdom I need so I can contend with the devil. He is an extraordinary enemy, and I want to be able to use my spiritual armor to gain victory in my life, within the body of Christ, and even in my dealings with the unbelieving world. And blessed Spirit, I truly desire to walk in Your power to bring glory to my Father, to my Lord, and to You. Amen.

Chapter 3

JESUS'S DEPENDENCE ON THE HOLY SPIRIT

TRINITY—AN EASY WORD TO say, but a hard concept to explain. We are to accept by faith the truths that God's Word reveals to us. This doesn't mean we will fully understand them, but it does mean we accept them as absolute truth and strive to live in light of them. Please don't miss what Paul is saying below in Philippians 2, for it is directed to us to copy in our lives. Our striving must be as we rest in the Holy Spirit's leading.

As I think about depending upon someone, I am reminded that my dependence upon the Holy Spirit must be at the heart of my walk of faith. For those of us

who know Jesus Christ as our personal Savior, our faith should increasingly deepen as His dependence upon the Holy Spirit becomes clearer to us. What follows in this chapter should just heighten our appreciation and love for what our Lord did on our behalf, to bring salvation to us.

Unlike the beginning of other chapters in this book, this isn't a story; it is a brief consideration of just how much our Lord loves you. As you're going to see, He emptied Himself to become the perfect sacrifice. But what so many don't see is how He absolutely depended upon the Holy Spirit, just as we are supposed to be doing. Get ready to see the depth of His love. Your attitude should be the same as that of Christ Jesus:

> Who, being in very nature God, did not consider equality with God something to be used to his own advantage; rather, he made himself nothing by taking the very nature of a servant, being made in human likeness. And being found in appearance as a man, he humbled himself by becoming obedient to death—even death on a cross! (Philippians 2:6–8)

Theologians refer to His making Himself nothing (v. 7) as the *kenosis*, which means "to empty." Yes, Jesus emptied Himself so He could be the perfect sacrifice for you and me.

One of the most thrilling truths to me has been discovering that while here upon the earth, Jesus also had to depend upon the Holy Spirit to live His life for the Father.

Can I explain how the Holy Spirit worked in Jesus's life? No, not any more than I can explain the Trinity. But if Jesus was to be the perfect human Redeemer, He had to be completely a man, like those He came to redeem (Hebrews 2:14–18). If we limit the Holy Spirit's ministry in Jesus's life, then it will certainly also limit what we allow Him to do in our lives. So please take in the truths of the following passages and more deeply value the extent of what Jesus gave up for us during His time here on earth.

> For he is sent by God. He speaks God's words, for God gives him the Spirit without limit. The Father loves his Son and has put everything into his hands. (John 3:34–35 NLT)

As our Redeemer, Jesus, too, had to depend upon the Holy Spirit to work in and through His life. In the NASB, Philippians 2:7 says that He "emptied Himself."

Let me try an imperfect illustration to explain this self-emptying. There is a young woman in my church who is an excellent harpist. Let's suppose she is going to travel with me to Africa. She will be leaving her harp behind, so she will not be able to play it while on our mission trip. Does she cease to be a harpist? No! She has merely set it aside for the time being. This is what Jesus did with His divine privileges. Can I further explain to you how He did this? No! But make no mistake: this is exactly what He did for you and me.

This is what Philippians 2 is trying to convey to us. He gave up His divine privileges so He could be more like us, also having to depend upon the Holy Spirit. By doing this, He became the perfect sacrifice—and the perfect example for us to follow.

Join me now in a brief, but very revealing, examination of how the Holy Spirit worked in the life of the man Jesus:

- It started with Mary. While she was still a virgin, she became pregnant through the power of the Holy Spirit (Matthew 1:18–19).
- In this next passage we see the Holy Spirit's coming: "As soon as Jesus was baptized, he went up out of the water. At that moment heaven was opened, and he saw the Spirit of God descending like a dove and alighting on him. And a voice from heaven said, 'This is my Son, whom I love; with him I am well pleased'" (Matthew 3:16–17).
- Then, to show Jesus's dependence upon the Holy Spirit and to show how the Spirit was personally working in Jesus's life, we read, "Then Jesus was led by the Spirit into the wilderness to be tempted by the devil" (Matthew 4:1).
- To further confirm the Spirit's control in Jesus's life, Luke writes, "Jesus returned to Galilee in the power of the Spirit, and news about him spread through the whole countryside. He was teaching in their synagogues, and everyone praised him" (Luke 4:14–15).

I am thrilled in my soul to read the next instance, when Jesus reveals most clearly what has taken place between Him and the Holy Spirit, just as it was predicted by Isaiah (Isaiah 61:1–11). This is lengthy, but it is invaluable on many levels in ministering to all who will drink it in.

He went to Nazareth, where he had been brought up, and on the Sabbath day he went into the synagogue, as was his custom. He stood up to read, and the scroll of the prophet Isaiah was handed to him. Unrolling it, he found the place where it is written: "The Spirit of the Lord is on me, because he has anointed me to proclaim good news to the poor. He has sent me to proclaim freedom for the prisoners and recovery of sight for the blind, to set the oppressed free, to proclaim the year of the Lord's favor." Then he rolled up the scroll, gave it back to the attendant and sat down. The eyes of everyone in the synagogue were fastened on him. He began by saying to them, "Today this scripture is fulfilled in your hearing." (Luke 4:16–21)

Next, please observe closely the following text, as Jesus's response to the charge of the Pharisees reveals the insight we must see:

And if I drive out demons by Beelzebul, by whom do your people drive them out? So then, they will be your judges. But if it is by the Spirit of God that I drive out demons, then the kingdom of God has come upon you. (Matthew 12:27–28)

So yes, even Jesus personally depended upon the Holy Spirit in His daily living. The perfect Lamb of God is once more our perfect example to follow.

Finally, Jesus didn't know God's timetable when He was here in the flesh:

> But about that day or hour no one knows, not even the angels in heaven, nor the Son, but only the Father. (Matthew 24:36)

I believe that the distinction between exegesis and eisegesis is at the heart of most errors and misunderstanding concerning the Scriptures. Exegesis is letting the Scripture speak for itself. The word comes from the Greek and means "to explain and lead you." The prefix "ex" means "out of." Eisegesis is making the Scripture say what you want it to say. The prefix "eis" comes from the Greek word for "into." Misinterpretation of the Scriptures is one of the reasons the Holy Spirit has been so misunderstood and all but ignored. Don't fall prey to the half-truths and blatant deceptions that thread their way throughout the Christian world.

What is our greatest defense? Each of us must remember that it is our personal responsibility to dig into the truth of God's Word. Listen to the words of the apostle Paul to Timothy, and please take them to heart:

> Study to shew thyself approved unto God, a workman that needeth not to be ashamed, rightly dividing the word of truth. But shun profane and vain babblings: for they will increase unto more ungodliness. (2 Timothy 2:15–16 KJV)

I ask you: If Jesus needed the Holy Spirit, how much more do we? I continue to be amazed at what is right before us in the Word of God, yet all too often it goes unnoticed. The word "workman" in the text above is an interesting word; it means "a toiler." Does this truly describe our efforts in studying the Word of God? To toil means to work at, to take time doing something, and to give effort in accomplishing a task.

I must admit that my own toiling in studying the Word of Truth has been, at times, too often hit-and-miss. How in the world can a believer take such an approach to the revealed will of the living God? As I look back, I realize that too much of my early life as a believer was spent preferring my own will over that of the One who knows best and loves me the most.

I am more convinced with each day that we do not appreciate all that has happened to us in becoming sons and daughters of our heavenly Father. As I write this, I am preparing to sing a song at church, accompanied on the piano by my daughter-in-law. The song, written by Bill Gaither, is titled "He Touched Me." Many know the words to it, but do we really give thought to all that has happened to us through being saved?

As a result of your salvation, do you know how He touched you and what part the Holy Spirit played? Please take the time to reflect on the following list of biblical truths, and you will more fully appreciate what has happened to you as a result of your salvation in Christ. In this list you will see some repetition. I have done this because each of us has a different vantage point, as we look at the Word of God. Over the years, as I have taught, time and again, I have seen individuals discover the same truth through different words.

I have been sanctified.
I have been justified.
I have been redeemed.
I was purchased.
I have been atoned.
I have been converted.
I have been regenerated.
I have been reconciled.
I am alive spiritually.
I am sealed by the Spirit.
I am able to discern spiritual things.
I was bought with a price.
I was brought out of the darkness.
I was brought into the light.
I am a new creation.
I have been reborn.
I am a child of the King.
I have been adopted.
I was made alive.
I am part of the family of God.
I became a babe in Christ.
I am a brother/sister in Christ.
I was lost and have been found.
I can talk with God.

Are you beginning to get the point of how essential it was that Jesus emptied Himself of His divine privileges so His sacrificial death could provide all this and more? Now back to the list of personal blessings:

I am part of the body of Christ.
I can have the mind of Christ.
I am a soldier of the cross.
I am more than a conqueror.
I can be filled with the Holy Spirit.

I can be led by the Spirit.

I can be empowered by the Spirit.

I can learn spiritual truths from the Spirit.

I can pray in the Spirit.

I am free from captivity.

I can walk in the light.

I have Christ as my Shepherd.

I can be holy.

I am now an heir to the kingdom.

I have been washed in the blood of Christ.

I have been given spiritual gifts.

I have eternal life.

I cannot lose my salvation.

I can seek those things that are above where Christ is.

I now know that my name is written in the Lamb's Book of Life.

I can now truly worship God.

When I don't know how to pray, the Holy Spirit prays for me.

I have the armor of God.

I am on the Victor's side.

I can intercede for you.

I have been delivered.

My sins have been forgiven.

I can put off the old man with his appetites.

I have received Christ.

I am now a priest.

I am important to the body of Christ.

You are important to me.

I am no longer in bondage.

I can glorify my God.

I can please my God.

Sin doesn't have to control me.

I can grow in the wisdom of God.

I can be faithful to God.

I can be renewed daily.
I am now righteous.
His promises are mine.
I have a ministry.
My resurrection to eternal life is certain.
I have a foretaste of my future life.
I am seated in heavenly places with Christ.
I have a real enemy, but he can only do to me
as I allow him.
I have victory over anxiety, worry, and fear.
I was saved from spiritual death and the wrath
of God.
I have been converted.
I am a partaker of the divine nature.
I have been cleansed.

Wow! Indeed, He touched me. In this current list, as it stands, there are about seventy examples of how He touched you. This list is not a complete list, so please see what you can add to it. Remember, we are in this together because Jesus came and fully emptied Himself to be our perfect Redeemer.

Let me end this chapter with two of the greatest prophecies of the Old Testament about our Savior and the relationship between Him and the Holy Spirit:

> Then a shoot will spring from the stem of Jesse, and a branch from his roots will bear fruit. The Spirit of the LORD will rest on Him, the spirit of wisdom and understanding, the spirit of counsel and strength, the spirit of knowledge and the fear of the LORD. (Isaiah 11:1–2 NASB)

The Spirit of the Sovereign LORD is on me, because the LORD has anointed me to proclaim good news to the poor. He has sent me to bind up the brokenhearted, to proclaim freedom for the captives and release from darkness for the prisoners, to proclaim the year of the LORD's favor and the day of vengeance of our God, to comfort all who mourn. (Isaiah 61:1–2)

As a man, Jesus was totally dependent upon the Holy Spirit—once again providing an example for us to follow. Because He emptied Himself, He was genuinely and personally confronted by Satan, and He later became the perfect sacrifice for humankind when He carried all the sin of the world upon Himself at Calvary.

I hope you will take your Bible and endeavor to look up each of the many ways Jesus and the Holy Spirit personally touched you as a result of your salvation. I hope, too, that you will appreciate that the Holy Spirit is the One who worked in you—and continues to want to work in you—to make all these blessings a reality.

Yes, all this and more is ours because of what Christ did on Calvary, but never forget how He depended on the Holy Spirit as He walked through this world as a man. Just as the Holy Spirit was there for Jesus, He is also there for you and me. He is waiting for us to humbly submit to His leading in our lives.

Prayer of Thanksgiving

Lord Jesus, Your sacrifice for me goes far beyond my ability to understand, but at the same time it clearly reveals to me the depth of Your love for me. I cannot find the words to thank You for setting aside Your divine privileges and depending completely upon the Holy Spirit in order to be that perfect sacrifice. Forgive me for not following You more faithfully. Please continue to pour Your tender mercies and grace into my life so I can become more like You in every aspect of my life. Please help me to more clearly see and understand the Holy Spirit's ministries in my life and become more dependent upon Him. Amen. Thank You, Lord.

Chapter 4

THE HOLY SPIRIT'S MINISTRY IN YOUR LIFE

IF THERE WAS SOMEONE in your life who wanted to help you at every turn, and even wanted to lead and empower you, would you not want him to do all of this?

Well, there is One, and He desires to do all of the above and so much more. He is your spiritual guide. Will you follow Him?

> The one who keeps God's commands lives in him, and he in them. And this is how we know that he lives in us: We know it by the Spirit he gave us. (1 John 3:24)

Several years ago, I took my two sons, Tim and Chad, to Washington, DC, and we went through the Smithsonian Museum. It was a great time together, but at the end of the day, I wished we would have had a guide to follow and listen to. As it was, we saw a lot, and I was very glad that my sons got to experience all that they did, but it could have meant so much more to them if a guide had been there taking us through and sharing all the history behind all we had seen.

You and I have a guide in the Holy Spirit—but are we aware of Him and all He desires to do in our lives? As you proceed through this chapter, first consider what He has already done for you. Then, with an open heart and mind, take in all that He still wants to do.

To say that the ministries of the Holy Spirit in the life of a believer are numerous falls far short of describing how invaluable He is to us. Here is the briefest of overviews, which I will expand upon:

- He sealed you when you believed (Ephesians 1:13).
- He has blessed you with the fruit of the Spirit (Galatians 5:22–23).
- He wants to fill you and empower you (Ephesians 5:18).

If this were all He wanted to do in our lives, we would still be victorious soldiers of the cross, but there is so much more He desires to do so we can be "more than conquerors" (Romans 8:37).

If you have never discovered the individual ministries

of the Holy Spirit in your life, consider just one chapter in the book of Romans as you begin this journey. Romans chapter 8 reveals sixteen ministries to us that the Holy Spirit desires to accomplish on our behalf.

"Blessed Spirit, how I love You." I have heard some believers say such words—and they are wonderful, beautiful, comforting words, yet when I continue to discuss the Holy Spirit, I so often discover that those who say such words often don't know the Holy Spirit very well. Please spend some discerning time in the following texts, letting your love for Him and your knowledge of Him grow. Even if you already have a vibrant relationship with Him, let the following quotes, right out of the New Living Translation of Romans 8, enrich your life:

1. And because you belong to him, the power of the life-giving Spirit has freed you from the power of sin that leads to death (v. 2).
2. Those who are dominated by the sinful nature think about sinful things, but those who are controlled by the Holy Spirit think about things that please the Spirit (v. 5).
3. So letting your sinful nature control your mind leads to death. But letting the Spirit control your mind leads to life and peace (v. 6).
4. But you are not controlled by your sinful nature. You are controlled by the Spirit if you have the Spirit of God living in you (v. 9).
5. And Christ lives within you, so even though your body will die because of sin, the Spirit gives you life because you have been made right with God (v. 10).
6. The Spirit of God, who raised Jesus from the dead, lives in you (v. 11a).

7. And just as God raised Christ Jesus from the dead, he will give life to your mortal bodies by this same Spirit living within you (v. 11b).

8. But if through the power of the Spirit you put to death the deeds of your sinful nature, you will live (v. 13).

9. For all who are led by the Spirit of God are children of God (v. 14).

10. Instead, you received God's Spirit when he adopted you as his own children (v. 15b).

11. Now we can call him, "Abba, Father" (v. 15c).

12. For his Spirit joins with our spirit to affirm that we are God's children (v. 16).

13. And we believers also groan, even though we have the Holy Spirit within us as a foretaste of future glory, for we long for our bodies to be released from sin and suffering (v. 23).

14. The Holy Spirit helps us in our weakness (v. 26a).

15. For example, we don't know what God wants us to pray for. But the Holy Spirit prays for us with groanings that cannot be expressed in words (v. 26b).

16. And the Father who knows all hearts knows what the Spirit is saying, for the Spirit pleads for us believers in harmony with God's own will (v. 27).

I ask you, are you intimately involved with this One who wants to do all these things for you? If not, then you are doing the very thing Paul challenges you not to do: "Do not grieve the Holy Spirit" (Ephesians 4:30).

The Bible tells us about many of the ministries of the Holy Spirit. If I were to comment on each of the texts that reveal His ministries, this book would be ten times as long. Instead, I want this book to be more basic— either as a starting point in your walk of faith or as a deepening tool for your walk of faith.

You might realize by now that I love lists of truths. Here is a list of some of the ministries of the Holy Spirit. To say He wants to help us is just too general of a statement. Look at some the specific ways He has helped and wants to help you and me:

> I am able to confess Jesus as my Lord only by Him (1 Corinthians 12:3).
> I was born to this new life in Christ by Him (John 3:6–8).
> He gave you the faith to believe (Romans 10:17).
> He adopted you into the family of God (Romans 8:15).
> He washed you in the blood of the Lamb (Hebrews 9:14).
> He sealed you (2 Corinthians 1:21–22).
> He indwells you (1 Corinthians 3:16).
> He baptized you (Acts 11:16).
> He freed you from sin to become like Him (2 Corinthians 3:12–18).
> He wants to lead you (Romans 8:14).
> He wants to empower you (Romans 15:13).
> He wants to cause you to remember (John 14:26).
> He wants to fill you (Ephesians 5:18).
> He wants to control you (Ephesians 5:18).
> He wants to help you put the old sinful nature to death (Romans 8:4–5).
> He prays for you (Romans 8:26–27).
> He wants to enrich your relationship with Christ and the Father (John 15:26).
> He wants to comfort you (John 14:16).
> He wants to use you to help restrain the iniquity that is already at work in the world (1

Corinthians 13:16 and 2 Thessalonians 2:7).
He wants to guide you into all truth (1 Corinthians 2:10–16).
He wants to reveal whatever the Father wants you to know (John 16:13–15).
He has made you the temple of God by dwelling in you (1 Corinthians 3:16).
He has blessed you with spiritual gifts (1 Corinthians 12:4–27).
He testifies to my spirit that I am a child of God (Romans 8:16).
He is the One who brought about my adoption (Romans 8:15).

He wants to help you in so many ways. This is not a complete list, but there is enough here for us to evaluate our relationship with the Holy Spirit. By doing this, we will be able to see how much we are grieving Him, instead of letting Him empower our lives. He is there for us and wants to have a relationship with us. We can depend on this One in our daily walk of faith, but we must let Him take the lead. Take the above list and look at each item in the list to see if what it says is real for you. If it is not, ask for His help to make it an active part of your life.

Come back to Paul's charge:

And do not grieve the Holy Spirit of God, with whom you were sealed for the day of redemption. (Ephesians 4:30)

First, what does this verse mean? "To sadden or distress" is at the heart of the word "grieve." It is not a new thing for human beings to grieve God, for again and again in the Old Testament we see humankind grieving God. Possibly the most astounding example comes from the time of Noah:

> The LORD regretted that he had made human beings on the earth, and his heart was deeply troubled. (Genesis 6:6)

In the above text, "deeply troubled" means "to bring pain to or cause to anger." In Ephesians 4:30, we see grief specifically coming from the third person of the Godhead, the Holy Spirit, who isn't just in the world, but is dwelling within us. What a dreadful sorrow our sin can bring against the One who lives within us and loves us so much!

What an extraordinary person the Holy Spirit is, and yet He is not given the personal honor He deserves. I pray you will take the time to consider the texts that declare who He is and what He wants to do in and through you. If these truths are already real for you, then please pray for your brothers and sisters in Christ, who have not yet discovered them.

Now I come to the topic that is truly the threshold we must cross in order to give free rein to the Holy Spirit's power in our lives. We all know about humility, but is it at the center of our character?

Humility is what sin has stolen from us. Satan does everything in his power to keep us from unbridling it in our lives. In the Old Testament, time and again we see that one of God's greatest desires for His people was humility. But because they were being controlled by sin, He had to take extraordinary steps to teach it to them. Consider these passages with me:

> Remember how the LORD your God led you all the way in the wilderness these forty years, to humble you and test you in order to know what was in your heart, whether or not you would keep his commands. (Deuteronomy 8:2)

The Bible declares that the Lord personally appeared to Solomon to give him this charge:

> If my people, who are called by my name, will humble themselves and pray and seek my face and turn from their wicked ways, then I will hear from heaven, and I will forgive their sin and will heal their land. (2 Chronicles 7:14)

Come with me to the New Testament and observe how humility is still what God is looking for in our lives. Only when we humble ourselves can the Holy Spirit freely step forward and take the lead in order to make us into who God desires us to be.

Once again, consider several passages.

> Don't be drunk with wine, because that will ruin your life. Instead, be filled with the Holy Spirit. (Ephesians 5:18 NLT)

The issue that is before us here is one of control. I chose this translation because it conveys to us the end of being controlled by strong drink—being ruined. This should emphasize to each of us the importance of what or who we allow to control our lives. What are you living for? What do you spend most of your time on? What is controlling your life right now?

Make no mistake—something or someone is always controlling each of us. If it is not the Holy Spirit, then our use to the Lord will be very limited. We must choose to let the Holy Spirit take control of our lives, and this takes humbling ourselves before the throne of grace to bring it about. Come with me, and let's examine one of the texts from the apostle Peter:

> Likewise you younger people, submit yourselves to your elders. Yes, all of you be submissive to one another, and be clothed with humility, for "God resists the proud, but gives grace to the humble." Therefore humble yourselves under the mighty hand of God, that He may exalt you in due time, casting all your care upon Him, for He cares for you. (1 Peter 5:5–7 NKJV)

This involves decisive acts of our wills.

"Submit yourselves." This means to subordinate yourself, to look upon others as being more important than yourself.

"Be clothed with humility." This means to put on modesty/restraint.

Now that we have received God's grace, we are ready to present ourselves to God. I must note here how the apostle Paul is an example for each of us to follow in our walk of faith. I am firmly convinced this is why Paul wrote all that he did in the New Testament. He put everyone else before himself, just as his Lord had done.

> I am less than the least of all the Lord's people. (Ephesians 3:8)

This was Paul's heart attitude, and it needs to be ours too. Paul is not belittling himself by saying what he did, but he is placing himself in the complete care of the Holy Spirit. Look at one more of the Bible's commands:

> Humble yourselves, therefore, under God's mighty hand, that he may lift you up in due time. (1 Peter 5:6)

The meaning here is to give your heart to God and wait upon Him for everything you need. Let this settle in until it becomes your truth. The Holy Spirit desires to fill you and control your life. It is here that your walk of faith is energized by Him.

I mentioned earlier that we must be careful not to follow our feelings instead of what the Word of God says. I want to balance that out by saying that our feelings do have their place, and more of us need to convey to others how we feel because of what God is doing for us.

Ultimately, the filling of the Spirit comes down to the Word of God and how much you are relying on it. It is a complete dependence upon and following of the One who wants to lead you. Jesus said that the Holy Spirit would teach us the truth, and through that truth, we can see His leading. You'll see this more clearly in the beginning of chapter 7.

There is much more I could say, but I would rather have you personally rely upon Him and allow Him to continue to lead you on your spiritual walk. This has been His desire from the moment He entered in and sealed you.

Words of Warning!

As you strive to surrender and allow the Holy Spirit to take the lead, never forget the Three Ds: distract, defeat, and discourage. You have an Enemy who will do all he can to distract you, defeat you, and discourage you in your personal efforts to be led by the Spirit. As I look back on my own journey and on that of other believers, I see how Satan and his minions tried to keep us from being successful. Just remember to get into the Word, and let the Word get into you. Then you will remember to put on the spiritual armor and make use of it daily. The Three Ds cannot stand up to the shield of faith and the rest of the armor of God. Why? Because this is what our Father desires for us.

We are far from done with this subject of humility. We'll come back to it in chapter 7. For the time being, let the truths in the following verses guide and keep you:

So I say, walk by the Spirit, and you will not gratify the desires of the flesh. For the flesh desires what is contrary to the Spirit, and the Spirit what is contrary to the flesh. They are in conflict with each other, so that you are not to do whatever you want. But if you are led by the Spirit, you are not under the law. (Galatians 5:16–18)

Prayer of Forgiveness

Blessed Spirit, I know I have grieved You through my ignorance and my preoccupation with myself and the world. Please forgive me and help me to humble myself under Your loving guidance, so You can accomplish all You desire to do through me. Amen.

Chapter 5

THE PRICELESS ARMOR OF GOD

YEARS AGO I WAS speaking at a Missions Conference in Mexico. My church had supported our missionaries, the Hornbrooks, for years, and they invited me to come and speak to a group of missionary families who were on a week's break. One of my subjects was the Armor of God.

One evening I encouraged all the children to be sure to be there the next morning with their parents because I wanted to show them how to put on the armor. As we closed that evening session, I asked if they had any questions.

Then it happened—one of those once-in-a-lifetime

experiences took place. A ten-year-old boy raised his hand and asked the following question: "Why would you take your armor off at night?"

That simple question from a child put everything into perspective. I answered, "No, I don't take off the armor at night. I just make sure I take the time in the morning to thank God for it and to remind myself what is available to me for the upcoming day."

Do you live by the Word of God, or do you just make use of it when you are backed into a corner? Don't be too quick to answer this.

If we say we are committed to something, that means it is a guiding force in your life. As it directs you to do something, you follow its lead and do as it says to do. Is this the way you relate to the Word of God?

If you answered yes to my question, then let me ask you another question: Do you daily equip yourself with the armor of God, or is it just a portion of the Word that you know about and maybe even have memorized, yet do little to become efficient in its use?

We have already considered our Enemy and some of his schemes. Now look closely at the armor that the Holy Spirit has provided for you so you can defend against every assault that Satan may hurl at you. Since the armor is so important, there is a strategic text. Please join me in seeing what the apostle Paul, moved by the Holy Spirit, shares in these verses to help us be more than conquerors in our encounters with ordinary people and with the spiritual wickedness in our world:

Finally, be strong in the Lord and in his mighty power. Put on the full armor of God, so that you can take your stand against the devil's schemes. For our struggle is not against flesh and blood, but against the rulers, against the authorities, against the powers of this dark world and against the spiritual forces of evil in the heavenly realms. Therefore put on the full armor of God, so that when the day of evil comes, you may be able to stand your ground, and after you have done everything, to stand. Stand firm then, with the belt of truth buckled around your waist, with the breastplate of righteousness in place, and with your feet fitted with the readiness that comes from the gospel of peace. In addition to all this, take up the shield of faith, with which you can extinguish all the flaming arrows of the evil one. Take the helmet of salvation and the sword of the Spirit, which is the word of God. And pray in the Spirit on all occasions with all kinds of prayers and requests. With this in mind, be alert and always keep on praying for all the Lord's people. (Ephesians 6:10–18)

Are you ready to either fine-tune the use of your armor or to make that special spiritual discovery that will change your life forever?

Look at the following brief but important overview of the above passage. I believe this will help you in preparing for what follows in this chapter. Let's start with verses 10–11:

"Finally" is one of those connecting words in grammar. So what is Paul saying? In light of all that he had already said in the first five chapters of Ephesians, now it was time to give his undivided attention to the spiritual armor.

"Be strong in the Lord and in his mighty power" is as clear as it gets—if we are listening. Are you ready to rely absolutely upon Him? Otherwise, you'll be fighting in your own strength and not His.

"Put on the full armor of God" is another imperative to every believer. This is a spiritual battle that we are in, and therefore it cannot be fought with physical armor. God has provided everything we need in His spiritual armor.

I have discovered through thirty-five years of counseling Christians and fellowshipping with other pastors and spiritual leaders, that most Christians do not use all the armor of God—and some Christians do not use any of it. So please take these truths into your life with the goal of proficiently utilizing them daily. Of course, if you are already using them, then I hope I can help fine-tune your skills for the battle.

Now back to our text:

You are to put on the armor of God "so that you can take your stand against the devil's schemes" (v. 11). This is the promise of the Holy Spirit's power. Notice that our responsibility is to stand (v. 13), but not until we have on all the armor of God. With His armor, we can take a stand against our Enemy, and no matter how he comes at us (trying to overwhelm us, trying to deceive us, trying to distract us, etc.), we will remain standing.

Don't miss what comes next:

"Our struggle is not against flesh and blood" (v. 12). Who is our battle against? Ultimately, we are not fighting against other people, but against Satan and his fallen demons as they use their powers and influence against us. You and I must have a Christian worldview. This means that as we look at the world and evaluate all that is taking place, our vantage point must be established by what the Bible teaches.

In our main passage in this chapter (Ephesians 6:10–18), we can see that although it often seems as if our battle is with humankind, this is not really the case. There are great negative spiritual influences taking place upon and through every aspect of the world around us. As we look at what is going on, we have to see things from God's perspective and not just from our own limited human understanding.

Yes, the people of this world (even including other believers in the church) can and will attack us, but we cannot allow ourselves to be sidetracked by these attacks. In dealing with the unbelieving world's attacks, our walk of faith must keep us strong. We must understand the condition of our attackers in order to best respond. They are lost, they are blind to the truth, they love darkness more than light, and in their depravity they are living for themselves without even realizing that Satan is utilizing them.

As far as the attacks from other believers, we can never forget that we all are part of the body of Jesus Christ, yet we can still fall prey to our old nature's appetites. This is where grace, mercy, love, and forgiveness come into our walk of faith. Remember, we are all sinners saved by grace, and whether we are dealing with the lost or with fellow believers, we must humbly place ourselves under the care of the Holy Spirit. As we do so, we must always keep our eyes on the real Enemy, or we will miss our calling to stand for the Gospel of Peace.

What follows are the ABCs of the pieces of spiritual armor. Carefully look at these so you can picture them in your mind as you walk through the day.

The six pieces of the armor of God.

The Belt of Truth

We must remind ourselves that we are to be walking in the truth (by both knowing God's truth and being truthful people). Walking in His truth gives us a solid foundation upon which we can stand.

To show you how central the truth is intended to be, notice that several other pieces of armor were attached to the Roman soldier's belt. We must be truthful and not give Satan a foothold in his fight against us. The Truth is essential in all that we do.

You and I live in a world of darkness, where lying is a way of life. As we walk in and share the truth, we will impact the world around us and will challenge other struggling believers to do the same. A truthful person stands out.

Before we move on, here are just a few practical insights:

- Every believer can stand *on* the truth because they are saved. This is simply believing that there is truth.
- Every believer can stand *for* the truth because they are saved. This is speaking truth to others—usually just other believers.
- We must also stand *in* the truth. This is when we live it throughout our lives on a regular basis. As a result, we are changed by the truth, and we make it our goal to change others through our daily living the truth.

The Breastplate of Righteousness

We must remind ourselves daily that Christ's righteousness is ours to walk in because of what He has done for us and in us. This is just some of what the truth reveals to us. Righteousness lets our Enemy know that we know to whom we belong, and that Satan therefore no longer has any claim upon us. But you and I must resolve to realize we are righteous. To be righteous means to walk in "rightness," to walk as Jesus walked. Satan knows full well that we are righteous. The ongoing issue will be for us to fully appreciate it and live in the light of it.

The Preparation of the Gospel of Peace

This is one of the greatest truths we must remember. We are to be peacemakers. We daily face an Enemy who is a destroyer and who strives to bring nothing but confusion and turmoil throughout our world. Peace will keep us settled, centered, and focused upon the battle and upon our real Enemy, so we will be able to see through all the various means he utilizes to fight against us and the Church.

If we are faithfully walking in the peace of the truth, our focus will not be distracted from what is actually taking place, and we will know how best to spiritually respond.

The Shield of Faith

With the shield of faith, you can quench all the Enemy's fiery darts. As we move to this fourth piece of armor, please note the first words introducing the shield of faith in Ephesians 6:16 (KJV): "Above all." This is intended to grab our full attention, for the Spirit

wants us to see how essential our faith is in each piece of armor and in using it in the spiritual battle. Without a grounded, growing faith in the Word, the Enemy will have the upper hand in the battle.

The word for "shield" here refers to a shield that is the size of a door. This is one of the pieces that could be hooked on to the Roman soldier's belt. As a result of being fastened to the belt, some of the weight of the shield would be taken off his arm as he held it. This greatly aided the soldier in being able to proficiently fight.

It is also important that we briefly consider what kind of evil darts are being shot at us. Just as coming in contact with something that is flammable can cause that material to be ignited and burn, so too, can spiritually evil fiery darts ignite our old nature and its appetites. It is our faith that separates us from those who are spiritually dead, and it gives us the complete victory over Satan and his demons.

The Helmet of Salvation

In this section about the helmet of salvation, I want to take the time to let you see just how all-inclusive all these pieces of armor are. I hope to motivate you to study God's Word to discover all you can about each of the other pieces.

The Roman soldier's helmet helped protect him from physical head trauma. Our minds are the key targets of the Enemy. The following list is to help you realize what the helmet represents for you in your mental and spiritual protection. This list is made up of the individual blessings from the Holy Spirit due to the gift of salvation. Yes, you have already seen this list in chapter 4, but I am repeating it here to drive home the reality of all that is represented by the helmet and is there for us to draw from for our personal mental protection. When you put on your helmet, you should be deeply encouraged and empowered by it.

He drew you out of the darkness.
He gave you the faith to believe.
He adopted you into the family of God.
He washed you in the blood of the Lamb.
He sealed you.
He indwells you.
He baptized you.
He freed you from sin.
He wants to lead you.
He wants to empower you.
He wants to cause you to remember.
He wants to fill you.
He wants to control you.
He wants to help you put the old sinful nature to death.
He prays for you.
He wants to enrich your relationship with Christ and the Father.
He wants to comfort you.
He wants to use you to help restrain the iniquity that is already at work in the world.
He wants to guide you into all truth.
He wants to reveal whatever the Father wants you to know.

He made you the temple of God by dwelling
in you.
He has blessed you with spiritual gifts.

I hope now you realize the power of having on the
full armor of God. You'll never be able to power up spiritually unless you bring these precious blessings into your
life as a practical part of your walk of faith.

The Sword of the Spirit

This piece of armor, the sword of the Spirit, is the
Word of God. Our testimony is important, but the
power of our words is found not in our experiences, but
in the Word of God. The better you know the Word, the
sharper your personal sword will be as you wield it in
your daily battles against Satan and his minions.

In Matthew 4, we observe the three temptations
(fiery darts) of Satan against Jesus as Satan attacked the
humanity of Christ. Jesus clearly responded to each
temptation with the Word of God—His sword of the
Spirit. The Word is where the power is, just waiting for
us to make use of it. So once again, look to Jesus as your
example to follow in your daily battles.

As we stand with our armor on fending off the wiles
of the devil, we are to "pray in the Spirit on all occasions
with all kinds of prayers and requests. With this in mind,
be alert and always keep on praying for all the Lord's
people" (Ephesians 6:18). Please—don't miss this invaluable action on our part. Prayer! Do you remember how
many times Jesus went off by Himself and prayed? It was

a way of life for Him, and it must be a way of life for us. Over the years in ministering to fellow Christians, I have regularly heard how they set aside a special time each day for praying. That's fine, but the battle praying here is to be almost like our breathing. With the armor on, as soldiers in the body of Christ, we are to be in constant communication with our God. This is especially true in our interaction with the Holy Spirit. What I have seen is that God's people use their own intellect, wisdom, and/or experience to maneuver through their daily battles instead of asking for the Spirit's leading and then following Him. As you will see in chapter 8, praying in the Spirit is a result of spending ample time in God's Word in order to learn His ways and means for defeating our enemy and helping each other.

The battle is real and the Enemy is real, but don't ever forget that as believers we are in this together. An essential part of our daily battle is praying for each other.

Remember Paul's words of confidence: "In all these things we are more than conquerors through him who loved us" (Romans 8:37). We can stand assured that we are on the Victor's side, but we must use the armor of God, as we fight the daily battles for Him and His Church. We have an Enemy who attacks from every direction and in ways we would never conceive, so be sure you remind yourself every morning that the armor is yours—and be ready to use it at all times.

Lastly, I want to make sure that each of us, as soldiers of the cross, know what our ultimate action must be as we have on the complete armor of God. We find this in our text:

> Therefore put on the full armor of God, so
> that when the day of evil comes, you may be
> able to stand your ground, and after you have
> done everything, to stand. (Ephesians 6:13)

Our duty is to stand. We don't attack or contrive any special plans; we stand. We do utilize each piece of the armor, but we do it as we stand in place as representatives of the King of Kings.

Having on the armor conveys an overwhelming picture to our Enemy that we know we are more than conquerors. Remember, the Enemy knows that the fully armored soldier of the cross is more than equipped to contend with anything he can try to do. But do *we* know it?

As you finish this chapter, know that as a brother or sister in Christ, your armor is priceless to you and to the rest of the body of Christ. We are in this together!

> But you, brothers and sisters, are not in dark-
> ness so that this day should surprise you like
> a thief. You are all children of the light and
> children of the day. We do not belong to the
> night or to the darkness. So then, let us not be
> like others, who are asleep, but let us be awake
> and sober. For those who sleep, sleep at night,
> and those who get drunk, get drunk at night.
> But since we belong to the day, let us be sober,
> putting on faith and love as a breastplate, and
> the hope of salvation as a helmet. (1 Thessalo-
> nians 5:4–8)

Prayer of Thanksgiving and Rejoicing

> *Father,* thank You for all Your provisions so I can be victorious today. Jesus, I praise Your name for winning the victory for me. Blessed Holy Spirit, please take these pieces of armor and make them real to me as You empower them. I know I can accomplish all You have in store for me for this day. Amen.

My Daily Appreciation of the Armor

Please accept the following as a practical suggestion for your daily prayer routine for the armor of God. I don't pray for each piece every day. In fact I usually take just one and thank God for His special piece of armor and my appreciation for it. As I go through each piece in prayer, I don't do all of them every morning; in fact, I usually do just one, but I want to give you an example of each piece and my appreciation for them.

> *Good morning, Lord.* Thank You for your faithfulness to me. I especially thank You for the armor You have given me.
>
> Lord, thank You for the belt of truth. Help me today to be truthful—to stand *for* the truth, to stand *on* the truth, and to stand *in* the truth—so I am ready to share Your truth and have it as my foundation.
>
> Lord, thank You for the breastplate of righteousness. Please remind me throughout today that when the Enemy looks at me, he clearly sees that I belong to You as he sees Your righteousness. Help me remember that I am

to walk in Your righteousness and not in my old nature.

Lord, thank You for the shoes of the gospel of peace. Continually remind me of how I am to be a peacemaker. My old nature wants to take sides, but as a peacemaker I must rest completely in the knowledge of the truth. Blessed Spirit, lead me in taking my stand for peace today. You have brought peace into my life and have given me the blessed opportunity to spread that peace throughout my world today. Thank You.

Lord, thank You for the shield of faith. As I walk in this fallen world today, please remind me that it is my biblically grounded faith that will make a difference in others' lives. You tell me that this shield is able to quench every one of Satan's fiery darts. That one great truth encourages me and helps me see how powerful my faith can be as I walk with You.

Lord, thank You for the helmet of salvation. As I approach this day, please continue to remind me of the more than seventy blessings my helmet represents. My life in You is to be extraordinary—not because of who I am, but because of whose I am—and the fact I am now a new creation in You. If I utilize your armor today, I will be more than a conqueror.

Lord, thank You for the sword of the Spirit. As I look at how Jesus handled each one of Satan's temptations, it reveals two great truths: (1) Satan refuses to accept that he is already defeated, and (2) Jesus has an absolute confidence in the truth. This same truth has been entrusted to my care, so please help me

get into the Word, and let the Word get into me, so I am ready for today's battle.

Father, guide me through this day as I depend more upon Your provisions and less upon my own human understanding. Help me to be a blessing by being a warrior for the cross. I pray this in my Savior's name. Amen.

Chapter 6

OUR IMPORTANCE
TO THE WORLD TODAY

I RECENTLY HAD ONE OF those do-nothing days. You know—when the sun isn't shining, it's cold outside, and you just can't seem to get anything accomplished. In the evening, I looked back over the day and was quite disappointed in myself.

Why? Because I know God has so much He wants to do through my life. Once more, join me and see the mighty things you and I can accomplish, even when we don't think we are up to the task.

I look back over my time in the Air Force and continue to be amazed at all God did through my life and the lives of other believers. As you probably know, the military is a very structured organization. Authority is everything, so most people—no matter their age or rank—make sure they don't step out of their place in the structure of things.

It was very moving to see the Holy Spirit utilize us as believers, no matter what our rank. No, we didn't go against the authority structure, but we did make a stand for the Lord. How did we do this? We followed our Lord by being gracious in our responses. Time and again, this proved to be a very powerful instrument in God's armament. Instead of responding through our emotions, we did all we could to be gracious, longsuffering, and encouraging to those in authority.

Christians can be confronted by any situation in life, and as we depend upon the Lord, we can respond with grace and get the attention of the most abrasive people.

During this time in the Air Force, unbelievers would often take advantage of their authority and abuse others with it. Once at a long, drawn-out meeting, a colonel came down hard and heavy on one of my fellow officers, but instead of responding in like manner, the officer took it in stride and responded with these gracious words: "Sir, I would be glad to check into that just as soon as our meeting is over."

After that meeting, he did exactly that, and he went to the colonel and gave him his report. The rather arrogant colonel responded, "I am not used to how you handled this. I want to thank you for getting this information, and I look forward to working with you." This opened the door for my Christian brother to further minister to the colonel as time went on.

You and I are very important to the Lord as we go out into our everyday walk, and the Holy Spirit wants to help us to be living testimonies for Christ.

We have already seen that the Holy Spirit lives within us, and that makes us the temple of God (1 Corinthians 3:16–17; 6:19; 2 Corinthians 6:16).

Have you ever asked yourself, "Why am I here? Why didn't God just take me home after I was saved?" I believe He has several reasons for not taking us home. Let's consider two of the most important ones. Please examine these insightful words from Paul:

> For the secret power of lawlessness is already at work; but the one who now holds it back will continue to do so till he is taken out of the way. (2 Thessalonians 2:7)

This is one of the main reasons you and I are here today. We are the light of the world, and our input is essential in restraining evil. He who is empowering us is the Holy Spirit, working in and through us! We know that the Holy Spirit dwells in each of us who make up the body of Christ. Corporately, we are intended to be the church, interacting with the world we live in. Again, we are being utilized by God to restrain the iniquity that is already at work in our world. As we look at the end-times, we know that the rapture of the church will take place, and this, my friend, will be when the Holy Spirit is "taken out of the way," because He dwells in us.

No, He won't leave the world, but His ministry will be somewhat different in the end times. He will still be needed, for there are going to be many that will come to Christ in those end times and they will need Him just as we have. But the current Body of Christ will be taken home to glory. As you read Paul's writings, you can see that they further confirm why we are here and why we must put off the old self and put on the new self (Ephesians 4:22–24; Colossians 3:9), and use the Armor of God (Ephesians 6:10–17). As we do this, the Holy Spirit is working through us to hold back the influence of iniquity, which Satan is energizing around the world. Paul declares that the Holy Spirit is at work in each individual believer as we utilize the spiritual gifts that He has provided for us.

> For the perfecting of the saints, for the work of the ministry, for the edifying of the body of Christ. (Ephesians 4:12 KJV)

So are you important, or are you just passing through until you go home for eternity? I sincerely hope it is crystal clear to you what should be taking place in our lives—and why. We were sanctified (made holy) at the moment of salvation, through the blood of Christ. But as we see in Paul's writings, there is an ongoing further sanctification taking place as we live by faith. Our personal challenge is to put off the old self and put on the new self, as we walk in our faith.

I won't be doing this very often, but in this chapter I utilize two lengthy scriptural quotes. Look at this extended text from Ephesians, and take in the fullness of its teaching. Here is confirmation of what I have been saying:

> Throw off your old sinful nature and your former way of life, which is corrupted by lust and deception. Instead, let the Spirit renew your thoughts and attitudes. Put on your new nature, created to be like God—truly righteous and holy. So stop telling lies. Let us tell our neighbors the truth, for we are all parts of the same body. And "don't sin by letting anger control you." Don't let the sun go down while you are still angry, for anger gives a foothold to the devil. If you are a thief, quit stealing. Instead, use your hands for good hard work, and then give generously to others in need. Don't use foul or abusive language. Let everything you say be good and helpful, so that your words will be an encouragement to those who hear them. And do not bring sorrow to God's Holy Spirit by the way you live. Remember, he has identified you as his own, guaranteeing that you will be saved on the day of redemption. Get rid of all bitterness, rage, anger, harsh words, and slander, as well as all types of evil behavior. (Ephesians 4:22–31 NLT)

Please take the time to make up a list of personal challenges from the above text (there are more than a dozen). Make it your list of daily personal goals as you call upon the Holy Spirit for His teaching, guiding, directing, filling, empowering, and enlightening—to become all that our Father wants you to be.

At this point in our country's history, we are seeing

things my generation has not seen before. Yes, all across the world, things have been becoming much worse for a long time. Since the fall of humankind, evil has been here, but not to the extent that we see it now in the United States. Whether you know it or not, the apostle John declared all the way back in the first century that he was in the end-times (1 John 2:18).

So here we are, and the end is nearer yet. I don't know if that means Christ will return this year or one hundred years from now, but we cannot ignore evil's reality. It is spreading, and we are to help stop it by cooperating with the Spirit of God working through us.

To further confirm where we are, tell me if what follows is not currently the case right here in the United States of America:

> But mark this: There will be terrible times in the last days. People will be lovers of themselves, lovers of money, boastful, proud, abusive, disobedient to their parents, ungrateful, unholy, without love, unforgiving, slanderous, without self-control, brutal, not lovers of the good, treacherous, rash, conceited, lovers of pleasure rather than lovers of God—having a form of godliness but denying its power. Have nothing to do with such people. (2 Timothy 3:1–5)

The above text is a clear description of what has been the norm for a long time in many countries around the world, but it is also now a word picture of what is taking place here in America. No, America has not been spotless since its founding—far from it. But because the Word was very central to our Founding Fathers, the principles in our founding documents placed God at the center of governmental affairs. Our country, like all others, is made up of sinful people, many whom are only looking out for their own best interests. No, we are not at the center of the end-times, but there is a definite shift taking place, even within the churches of America. This should just further drive home the point that you and I, empowered and led by the Holy Spirit, are very much needed in today's world. So let's move on to the essential work at hand, which is to be accomplished through us as we humble ourselves to the Holy Spirit.

Let's now consider another point from the Scriptures:

> For the mystery of lawlessness is already at work; only He who now restrains will do so until He is taken out of the way. (2 Thessalonians 2:7 NKJV)

Don't miss this great truth. All that Paul and Peter write about regarding our changing and growing into a more Christlike person is meant to make us the most efficient, righteous people we can be. Through this, we acquire a Christian worldview, enabling us to see the spiritual reality of what is before us.

Again, second Thessalonians 2:7 describes the Holy Spirit as "He who now restrains." How is the Holy Spirit restraining? He dwells within each of us who are genuine born-again believers. We are the church of the living God, and as such, God has chosen us to interact in this world to bring forth the kingdom of God among other people. Now that Jesus is at the right hand of God the Father, the task of preparing this world for His second coming is on our shoulders as we allow the Holy Spirit to empower our lives through our walk of faith.

Are those around you who are still lost and living under the power of Satan seeing something different in your life as you respond to the evil that so saturates their world today? As I have already said, we are the light in this world (Matthew 5:14; Ephesians 5:8). The question is: How brightly are we shining? Is the world seeing Christ and His ways in us through the light of our lives?

We must see that we are greatly needed by God. The individual believers in the church, empowered by the Holy Spirit, are to restrain the evil that is currently saturating our world. By being utilized by the Spirit, we gain a healthy Christian worldview, so our light will shine brighter in the darkness of this world.

So what is a Christian worldview? It is being able to see reality, no matter what the situation, and this reality comes to us through knowing three great truths:

1. God the Father is seated on His throne.
2. Jesus, the risen Savior, is at God's right hand praying for us.
3. The Holy Spirit has sealed us and dwells in us, making us the temple of God.

With these three truths settled firmly in our heart of hearts, we can be sure that no matter what is going on in our world, God is in control and His plans will not be altered by the evil of mankind.

With all this in mind, what actions should we be taking?

- By this everyone will know that you are my disciples, if you love one another (John 13:35).
- Do not love the world or anything in the world (1 John 2:15).
- In your relationships with one another, have the same mindset as Christ Jesus (Philippians 2:5).
- Set your hearts on things above, where Christ is, seated at the right hand of God (Colossians 3:1).
- After you have done everything, . . . stand (Ephesians 6:13).

As we study and apply the Word, we will become more and more like our Lord. But how is all this—and more—to be accomplished? This brings us back to our relationship with the Holy Spirit—the third person of the Godhead. Remember, He came to dwell within each of us for a very special purpose: to make us an active temple of the living God. As the temple of God, we are to become more and more holy (1 Peter 1:15–16). While this takes place, He can then accomplish in and through our lives what He has desired to do all along.

We must be careful though, not to let this make us prideful, but rather we must become the humble servants He desires us to be. Just like the apostle Paul speaks of himself in Ephesians 3:8, we are to regard ourselves as "less than the least of all the Lord's people." Humility is the key that unlocks our doors of ministry.

If we are becoming more humble, we will more clearly see our importance in the world today. This may seem a bit contradictory to Paul's earlier statement of being "less than the least of all the Lord's people," but it really brings a balance into our spiritual understanding. Knowing our position in Christ (a humble servant) frees us up to be empowered by the Holy Spirit to be used as He pleases. If we don't, we will continue to stifle God in His desire to accomplish all He wants to accomplish through us. This is why chapter 7 is all about humility.

The second part of our importance to this fallen world is in proclaiming the Gospel of Christ to those around us. This was a truth the Lord laid upon my heart early in my life. I grew up in a very unbelieving family, but as I grew daily in the Lord, I was deeply burdened to share my faith in Christ. As I look back, I realize that I was shut down in my witnessing at almost every turn, but I never lost my desire to share Christ with my family and friends. In fact, this actually empowered me to search out new ways to share Christ with them.

The truth that the apostle Paul declares in Romans 8:16 must be firmly settled and established in our lives, and then we will be deeply burdened for the lost: "The Spirit himself testifies with our spirit that we are God's children."

We have the greatest gift of all: the gift of being eternally secure in Christ. We have this foundational gift because we have believed in what He did for us personally. When we grasp what He has done for us, we become more motivated to want to share this truth of all truths with everyone we can.

Have you or others you know ever been beaten over

the head with the gospel? This is where our being humble and open to the working of the Holy Spirit in our lives is essential. If we follow His leading, we will not blatantly offend unbelievers with the truths of God's Word.

Let me continue to utilize the idea of a gift. You don't take a beautifully wrapped, expensive gift and then throw it at a person. No! Of course you don't. You put it out there in the most loving way that you can. Your personality or nature might be different from those of other people, but please don't let that make you feel less qualified to confidently give the gift.

This is just one of the many ways Satan attacks believers. He gets us to compare ourselves with other believers, and he often convinces us that we just aren't the right person to reach out with the gospel. Satan can get us to reason that we are too shy, or a hundred other reasons why we are not qualified to evangelize. This is why we must appreciate that with the Holy Spirit's empowering (letting Him take the lead as we follow Him), we, too, can win the lost to Christ.

Because of what Christ did in His life and then in His death upon the cross, He deserves nothing less than our best. We must let our light shine as brightly as we possibly can. Our relationship with and dependence upon the Holy Spirit will make us the best witnesses we can be. This is our Calling.

At this point, I want to share with you what I believe is the most powerful, revealing truth we have to offer the unbelieving world. John 3:16 is known by even the unchurched, but there is another passage that is incredibly powerful for our use in our personal outreach. Here it is in its entirety:

> We accept human testimony, but God's testimony is greater because it is the testimony of God, which he has given about his Son. Whoever believes in the Son of God accepts this testimony. Whoever does not believe God has made him out to be a liar, because they have not believed the testimony God has given about his Son. And this is the testimony: God has given us eternal life, and this life is in his Son. Whoever has the Son has life; whoever does not have the Son of God does not have life. I write these things to you who believe in the name of the Son of God so that you may know that you have eternal life. (1 John 5:9–13)

This is the clearest presentation in Scripture of what it means to be a Christian.

I ask you, can it be any clearer? After I share this passage with an unbeliever, my next step is to ask the person to tell me about their relationship with Christ, because that is what these five verses are all about. This has been one of the main reasons I have led so many people to Christ over the years. The passage is to the point, and it is clear. The unsaved either accept the present God has given (His Son), or they just leave it sitting there (beautifully wrapped in the truth, but unopened). Either way, they are left with a clear gospel message. Please see how the world needs us to both restrain evil and lead others to Christ.

As I bring this chapter to a close, I want to return to the idea of a Christian worldview. This way of seeing will develop in your life as you become more Christlike. As you put on the mind of Christ, you begin looking at everything from a different vantage point. Yes, our time in history is growing progressively worse, but if we examine all of this from the vantage point of the Father being seated upon His throne in glory, Jesus praying for us at His Father's right hand, and the Holy Spirit dwelling in us, we can see that all things are still under the complete control of God. God's perfect plan of the ages is still unfolding before us, and you and I have a vital part to play in bringing all of this about.

When we have this perspective on life, we will act and react to world events as we should, and the unbelieving world will see a great difference between their lives and ours.

I learned from my missionary friends that when it seems like your world is being turned upside down and spinning out of control, it is then that you draw closer to the Lord, by reminding yourself that the Father, Jesus the Lord, and the Holy Spirit are there with you, every step of the way. Rest in them, realizing you are important to them and that they have a plan for you to follow. This calms your soul and helps you understand what is going on. I have had missionary after missionary encourage me by telling me that this is how they have seen God's leading out on the mission field.

A supernatural calm and trust in God, during hard times, is powerful and practical living proof that you and

I are different and have something the rest of the world doesn't have. But to do this, we must be growing in our understanding and relationship with the Holy Spirit. Remember, He wants to lead us and empower us in our daily walk.

Because I have a Christian worldview, I find that I am much more settled, certain, and influential in the lives of others. I guarantee you that this will greatly empower the way you let your light shine in an ever-darkening world.

Three Great Truths to Think About

1. A good friend of mine, evangelist Norm Sharbaugh, gave me a great insight into Ephesians 5:18, which tells us to "be filled with the Spirit." He explained that when you are filled with the Spirit, you do not get more of the Holy Spirit; He gets more of you! This passage is speaking about who or what controls us. If we surrender ourselves to Him, He becomes more powerful in us, and God's will is wonderfully accomplished in and through our lives, and we don't get in the way of the truth.

2. All the above is couched in our being an active part of the body of Jesus Christ. Are you currently serving at your church? Are you fellowshipping with other believers? Are you praying for each other's needs? Do your neighbors and friends know where you are a church member? Don't ever forget the charge of the apostle Paul in Ephesians 4:16: "From him the whole body, joined and held together by every supporting ligament, grows and builds itself up in love, as each part does its work." You are invaluable to your church and to the rest of the body of Christ!

3. Make sure you continue in your walk of faith in the same way you started. "You received the Spirit because

you believed the message you heard about Christ. How foolish can you be? After starting your new lives in the Spirit, why are you now trying to become perfect by your own human effort? Have you experienced so much for nothing? Surely it was not in vain, was it?" (Galatians 3:2–4 NLT).

It is very easy to let the Word become nothing more than head knowledge instead of wisdom, to faithfully guide and direct us through our daily walk of faith. Let that new nature in you take the lead, as you follow the Holy Spirit.

Prayer of Forgiveness and for Power

Blessed Spirit, forgive me for the times I have quenched You and/or grieved You. Fill me with Your presence and empower me so I can be an effective instrument in Your hands. Thank You for Your longsuffering in my life. Help me to be the spiritual Christian You have wanted me to be from that first day You came into my life and sealed me. Help me to walk in Your strength instead of my own so that I will be accomplishing the will of God for myself and others and will truly impact this world for You. Amen.

Chapter 7

THE KEY TO ALL OF THIS: PERSONAL HUMILITY

AFTER I HAD BEEN at First Baptist Church for twenty-five years, the leaders asked my wife, Reta, how they might truly minister to me. Her response changed my life forever. She told them I would love to go to Israel, and so they sent me. I wish I could have done this thirty years earlier. In fact, if you are a pastor reading this, I cannot emphasize enough how going to Israel will change your life in the ministry.

Before I left for Israel, everyone was saying, "You'll get to walk where Jesus walked." But it wasn't until I got there and traveled through the Holy Land, that walking where He walked brought me to my knees. What an awesome privilege!

What does this have to do with humility? When our group of about twenty people got to Gethsemane and I was in the garden by myself, the Lord brought me to my knees—literally. I went away by myself and read the accounts from Matthew, Mark, and Luke of Jesus in that precious garden. My heart was broken like it had never been before. It was there for the first time that I truly understood what Jesus had done for me. And He did it all in absolute humility, wanting to accomplish His Father's will. What follows in this chapter flows out of my personal humbling experience, there in the garden of Gethsemane. My life has been so much richer since I saw my need for humility in my daily walk of faith.

The key behind personal humility is learning to let go (*Lord, I want Your will instead of mine*), but remaining engaged (I must be personally responsible). Humility is not about giving up anything, but it is to allow the Holy Spirit to truly take control of our lives to the point that we do the very thing Jesus was always trying to get His disciples to understand and do: "Then he said to them all: 'Whoever wants to be my disciple must deny themselves and take up their cross daily and follow me'" (Luke 9:23).

We don't become disengaged in life; quite the opposite, we become actively involved as we follow the Holy Spirit step by step, every day. Humility is easy to define, but is very difficult to consistently practice.

At the time I was going through seminary, the constant challenge brought before us was, "Who's on the throne of your heart?" The leaders of the seminary were

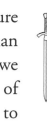

trying to get us to daily examine ourselves to make sure Jesus was truly the Lord of our lives. Now more than thirty years later, I believe a more practical question we need to answer for ourselves is, "Who's in control of your life—the Holy Spirit or you?" Yes, it is essential to have Jesus on the throne of our hearts, but if we are not willing to follow the One whom Jesus sent to take the lead in our lives, then we are still too much in charge.

As you look at your life today, who or what is in control of it? I am afraid that most of us don't give enough thought to this great truth—at least not until we come to one of those roadblocks or out-of-control situations. It's then that we discover, too late, that we were the one in charge and that we had not given the Holy Spirit His rightful place of leading us through the Word (John 16:13).

Scripture makes it very obvious that the Holy Spirit is the One we need to be following. It is He who teaches us about Christ and the Father and who leads us in the truth. Jesus is at the right hand of His Father praying for us, while the Holy Spirit is dwelling in us. This takes nothing away from our relationship with Christ, but it is certainly illuminating concerning our relationship with the Holy Spirit. Before you proceed, please consider these three passages: John 14:15–26, John 15:26, and John 16:12–15.

How do I best relate to you the idea of personal humility? I have given this a lot of thought, and I want to utilize two biblical examples to help establish a good understanding of what it means to be humble and yet still deeply involved. These examples are from Jesus and the apostle Paul.

Before we look at Paul, consider with me what it means to be humble and yet still deeply involved. To many people, being humble means to be passive, but we must see that this is not the case at all. Our Lord and Paul were both humble, yet were actively involved in all that was going on around them.

At the core of being humble is the idea of surrendering yourself. Webster's dictionary says that being humble means to "yield to the power, control, possession of another." The idea here is complete—not partial—surrender. To gain a well-balanced understanding, we see that biblical humility is not belittling oneself (Matthew 6:16–18; Romans 12:3), but is exalting or praising others, especially God and Christ (John 3:30; Philippians 2:3)—and yes, also the Holy Spirit (John 14–16). A humble person must focus more on God and others than on himself. One of the wonderful results of doing this is that we will further discover our new lives in Christ.

What we see is that true humility produces gratitude, and gratitude results in thanksgiving and even more dependence. Do you see this in your relationship with the Holy Spirit? Are you daily growing in your dependence upon Him?

As we have already seen in chapter 3, Jesus is always the One we need to look to as our example to follow. Before we look once more at Jesus, I want us to consider the apostle Paul and the amazing change that took place in his life.

In light of Christ's example in chapter 3, what should we give up of our free will each day to be more like Him? I believe this is what made Paul the powerful follower of Christ that he was, and this is why I use him as my first example. Paul uses the term "servant" (or "bond servant") to introduce himself in several of his epistles. The bond servant was one who had no rights—one who was fully surrendered to follow another. If you are like me, this is not something I readily do, even in my relationship with my Lord. The better I know the Scriptures, the more I realize how completely I must surrender myself and depend upon the Holy Spirit, so I can faithfully follow my Lord.

As I look at who and what Paul was before he was saved, I am convinced that his example should greatly encourage each of us, as we see how much we, too, can change by getting rid of the old self. Paul writes that previously he put his confidence in what human beings typically value:

> If someone else thinks they have reasons to put confidence in the flesh, I have more: circumcised on the eighth day, of the people of Israel, of the tribe of Benjamin, a Hebrew of Hebrews; in regard to the law, a Pharisee; as for zeal, persecuting the church; as for righteousness based on the law, faultless. But whatever were gains to me I now consider loss for the sake of Christ. (Philippians 3:4–7)

I hope you agree with me. Here was a surrendered man, and as a result, he was a greatly changed man.

Look at just one of these great changes that took place in Paul's life. He was formerly a Pharisee. Pharisees were fixed upon observing the law, and yet it was only an outward faithfulness, as their hearts were nowhere close to the righteousness of God. They were only concerned with getting people's praise. As a result, they looked down on others as worthless sinners. After Paul's salvation, his main concern was becoming Christlike and meeting the needs of others. What a profound change in Paul's character, showing us how much we also can change—as we, too, surrender ourselves to the Holy Spirit's control!

This is just one example of the amount of change that can take place in a believer's life after salvation. The extent to which we can change is unlimited. This all rests upon the freeing power of humility. Never cease to be engaged in life, but do cease to be someone who has to be in control. The humble person is the one who knows he is to become more like Jesus, as a result of each day's events—a person who puts on the mind of Christ.

If you are like me, you need to be able to see how you are changing and becoming more like Jesus. Here are some excellent questions to ask yourself along the way:

- Am I more thankful each day?
- Am I daily seeing new ways to praise God?
- Can I see more of Jesus's character in myself?
- Is it becoming more natural for me to be before the throne of grace?
- Am I loving all people more?
- Do I see more of the glory of God in His creation?
- Am I deeply concerned about the Holy Spirit and following His leading?

This list could go on and on, but there is enough here for us to use to examine ourselves. Are the qualities found in these questions a growing part of your everyday life?

Humility is truly our passport to greater things in the kingdom of God. As you grow in your humility, you will find that you can't believe you are doing things that are so Christlike. This is a sign that the Spirit is at work in you rather than you striving in your own strength. True humility releases the hold the old nature has on us.

Writing this book has been the greatest challenge of my life, and as I read back over it, I marvel at what the Holy Spirit has revealed to me. I cannot believe what I have discovered as I have put myself in His hands and have allowed Him to lead me in the truth and through each day's events.

God has given me a changed heart—one that continues to desire to be changed even more. As I said earlier in this book, I don't have all the answers, but what I do have is an awe-inspired soul that gives God the Father, Jesus the Son, and the Holy Spirit all the praise, honor, and glory. I pray that you'll join me as you keep a biblically balanced view of the Father, the Son, and the Holy Spirit.

Never forget these words of Jesus:

> But the Comforter, which is the Holy Ghost, whom the Father will send in my name, he shall teach you all things, and bring all things to your remembrance, whatsoever I have said unto you. (John 14:26 KJV)

I pray that this book will help you appreciate the Holy Spirit for who He is—God—and that you will therefore give Him praise, love, worship, honor, and all that is due Him, as you follow His lead.

As you do this, let me caution you as to how Satan may try to distort your relationship with the Holy Spirit. Our adversary has prompted some believers to exalt themselves into believing they can perform miracles, speak in spiritual tongues, and follow other paths that distort the truth. Rest and trust in the revealed truth of the Bible, as you faithfully follow the Holy Spirit's teaching and leading.

As I say this, let me make sure I present the full picture of what can still be taking place. A dear missionary friend of mine who is solidly grounded in the Word had this to share with me. He had a Christian brother on the mission field who was trying to reach out to a very isolated and lost group of people. He did not yet have a good grasp of their language, but on one occasion he was able to speak in their local language, and as a result, several were saved. He said this absolutely stopped him in his tracks and caused him to appreciate the Holy Spirit's ministry in his life, more than ever. Since that time, his friend has never done this again, but it greatly changed his life and deepened his dependence upon the Spirit of God.

Let me complete my picture of Paul's example of humility. We have already considered being surrendered, but there is another aspect involved in being humble before the Holy Spirit. We must fully appreciate who we are, what certainty we have in the future, and what can be accomplished through us as we become more humble.

Come back with me once more to Paul's changed life. In Philippians 3 we are given a wonderful example of what we can give up to be even more humble:

> But whatever were gains to me I now consider loss for the sake of Christ. What is more, I consider everything a loss because of the surpassing worth of knowing Christ Jesus my Lord, for whose sake I have lost all things. I consider them garbage, that I may gain Christ and be found in him, not having a righteousness of my own that comes from the law, but that which is through faith in Christ—the righteousness that comes from God on the basis of faith. I want to know Christ—yes, to know the power of his resurrection and participation in his sufferings, becoming like him in his death, and so, somehow, attaining to the resurrection from the dead. (Philippians 3:7–11)

As we are given this most visual word picture of what had taken place and what was still taking place at the core of Paul's life, freely given in behalf of knowing his Lord more intimately, I pray that each of us will see the power of surrendering ourselves and letting humility become our heart's desire.

Paul is a great example of humility, but our second and most important example is Jesus Himself. This is especially true regarding humility. Just think about what He did for you. In chapter 2 of Philippians, the Holy

Spirit reveals the greatest of truths in regard to Jesus's submission to His Father's will. We are told that Jesus emptied Himself of His divine privileges and placed Himself in the complete care of the Holy Spirit.

As I have grown in my understanding of this, my appreciation of and love for my Lord has greatly deepened. Jesus clearly surrendered Himself while He was here in His physical body, and the more we let the reality of this settle into our relationship with Him, the more we will come to urgently see our own need for Christlike humility. This amazing truth has greatly deepened my faith and has placed me in constant awe and reverence of Him. Please take in the fullness of the following text:

> And being found in appearance as a man, he humbled himself by becoming obedient to death—even death on a cross! (Philippians 2:8)

I want to begin with this verse because it is the foundation to all that follows, yet I am afraid it is one of those passages that we almost take for granted without much heartrending thought. So join me as I tie in some other great truths that demonstrate Jesus's humility.

> For even his own brothers did not believe in him. (John 7:5)

What must it have been like for Jesus to grow up with His brothers and for them to daily see His humility, unconditional love, giving spirit, and yet they did not believe in Him? Again, we see a humble, loving, always-giving man that you and I can freely follow.

We can appreciate Jesus even more when we hear Him say about His life, "No one takes it from me, but I lay it down of my own accord" (John 10:18). Jesus is speaking here of His death. He is making it crystal clear that He was choosing, as a man, to give up His life for us and for all the lost sinners out there who still need salvation.

Look at what Luke captures for us regarding the character of our Jesus:

> I have come to bring fire on the earth, and how I wish it were already kindled! But I have a baptism to undergo, and what constraint I am under until it is completed! (Luke 12:49–50)

As I said earlier, Jesus emptied Himself of His divine privileges, and as a result, even He didn't know the specific timing of the end-times, but He did know God's overall plan of the ages. He knew that He had to humble and surrender Himself to death on the cross so that the eternal plan could ultimately come to fulfillment. This was our Creator doing all of this for us, and as we join Him in the garden, we can see the real struggle that was taking place within His heart of hearts:

> He withdrew about a stone's throw beyond them, knelt down and prayed, "Father, if you are willing, take this cup from me; yet not my will, but yours be done." An angel from heaven

appeared to him and strengthened him. And being in anguish, he prayed more earnestly, and his sweat was like drops of blood falling to the ground. (Luke 22:41–44)

I want to end this chapter with this deeply emotional moment in Jesus's life. Here He was crying out to the Father, as anyone would do, while greatly distressed. In His flesh, it was beyond Him as to what was just ahead—so much so that His physical body, mind, and soul were being poured out there in Gethsemane. Let the reality of all this become yours in your relationship with Christ. You are His, only because of what He went through there in the garden and what followed on the cross.

I shared earlier of my time in the garden of Gethsemane. All this and more bore into the core of my being, as I really understood the humility of my Savior for the first time. I can honestly say that from that point on in my life I have deeply desired to follow the Holy Spirit's leading, and I continue to surrender to Him each day.

I could stop right here, and you would agree that Jesus was a humble man, stepping up on our behalf to change all eternity, but I want to make sure to bring all this into perspective, so that we will appreciate how important humility is for us.

Please take the time to let the significance of the following titles and names settle into your heart, and you will see the humility of Christ as you have never before seen it.

- Here was God (John 20:28).
- Here was the Lord (Matthew 22:43–44).
- Here was the Word (John 1:1, 14).
- Here was the Son of God (Luke 1:35).
- Here was the Ruler of God's Creation (Revelation 3:14).
- Here was the Alpha and Omega (Revelation 1:8).
- Here was the Captain of Salvation (Hebrews 2:10).
- Here was the Light of the World (John 8:12).
- Here was the Creator of All Things (John 1:3).
- Here was the Great High Priest (Hebrews 4:14).
- Here was the KING OF KINGS AND LORD OF LORDS (Revelation 19:16).

Once again, my list is not complete, but if you can walk away from the biblical presentation of the man Jesus, knowing full well who He was and realizing all He went through for you, and not see the absolute significance of His humility, then I encourage you to get to know Him more intimately.

Closing Thoughts

Please let the obvious surrendering of the apostle Paul and the humanity of Jesus settle into your heart of hearts, or you will miss your greatest examples to follow in your personal need for humility. Humility is what the Holy Spirit needs in us, in order to have full sway in our lives. Can there be anything more humbling than to know that you and I are now the temple of the living God? The Holy Spirit, by taking up residency in our lives, has made us so. Go forth each day with this amazing banner utmost in your heart and mind: "I am the temple of the living God, and so I have the opportunity to show God's glory in human form, to anyone and everyone I come in contact with today." That, my friend, is being Christlike.

Prayer of Great Concern

> *Precious Lord*, please pray for my humility in my relationship with the Holy Spirit. It is so easy to become prideful when we accomplish things for You. Let my greatest desire be that of being more like You, when You were here in the flesh, for then and only then can I let the Holy Spirit have full control of my life. Thank You, Lord. Amen.

Chapter 8

THE OBVIOUS IS NOT ALWAYS SO OBVIOUS!

IF I WERE TO stop here, it would be an injustice to what has driven me to write this book on the Holy Spirit. Stay with me a little longer, and I believe you will discover some very important practical insights into your personal relationship with the Third Person of The Godhead.

As I look back over my years of being a pastor, I see that much of my time was consumed by the needs of others. Pastors often find themselves just trying to keep up. Preaching the Word of God is a rich blessing, but it takes more than preaching to produce spiritual fruit in the believer's life. This is where you, as part of a church family, come in. Your pastor needs your faithful prayers, especially in effectively utilizing his study time and the time he needs to minister to individuals. Preaching and teaching take little time to actually do, but they take a lot of preparation time.

What takes place behind the scenes can easily devour your pastor's time. Such ministries as helping individuals (counseling, Bible study, personal help in whatever area of life is needed), trying to strengthen families (resolving conflicts, giving spiritual direction, establishing family time together), and the general church activities (building projects, training teachers, and the multitude of much-needed programs) take up much time. I hope you see why your prayers for your pastor are essential. And yes, your personal ministry is essential to the church family.

In the brief time a pastor has to preach and teach on Sundays and Wednesdays, it is easy for him to proclaim the Word and yet not give enough practical application. Over the years, I and other preachers have often preached messages with such commands as "Be filled with the Spirit," "Pray in the Spirit," and "Walk in the Spirit."

These three commands stand out as very important actions that we need to put into practice. And yet so often they are presented without clear explanation on how to do them. So join me as we continue on the last part of our journey of personal discovery and enrichment through our relationship with the Holy Spirit.

The Important Key

As I mentioned earlier, it's not that we get more of the Holy Spirit, but we give more of ourselves to Him. We are the temple, and He needs full access to all of the temple. This is why we must follow Jesus's example and completely humble ourselves. He set the example for us, giving His all to accomplish His Father's will. He was driven by His deep love for His Father and for all mankind.

> If ye keep my commandments, ye shall abide in my love; even as I have kept my Father's commandments, and abide in his love. (John 15:10 KJV)

If we are to follow His lead in humbling ourselves, we must keep the following truth ever present in our hearts and minds:

> If ye abide in me, and my words abide in you, ye shall ask what ye will, and it shall be done unto you. (John 15:7 KJV)

If this is true for us, then our love for Him will grow, and our dependence upon the Holy Spirit will become second nature to us as these two great truths energize our walk of faith.

To further drive home our need of dependence upon Him, consider these passages, letting the revealed truth fully impact your heart, mind, and soul:

> Don't you know that you yourselves are God's temple and that God's Spirit dwells in your midst? (1 Corinthians 3:16)
>
> If anyone destroys God's temple, God will destroy that person; for God's temple is sacred, and you together are that temple. (1 Corinthians 3:17)
>
> Do you not know that your bodies are temples of the Holy Spirit, who is in you, whom you have received from God? You are not your own. (1 Corinthians 6:19)
>
> What agreement is there between the temple of God and idols? For we are the temple of the living God. (2 Corinthians 6:16)

Please take the time to let this essential truth (that you are the temple) settle into the deepest folds of your heart. Once you do, you will see just how special you are to the Father and to the rest of the body of Christ. This won't come overnight; it is intended to be a lifelong growing experience.

Each of the commands that follow is intended to lead us deeper into our new life in Christ. With them we can be empowered to accomplish all that the Father desires for us. Let the following passage from Ephesians be a guide for you:

> Be very careful, then, how you live—not as unwise but as wise, making the most of every opportunity, because the days are evil.

> Therefore do not be foolish, but understand what the Lord's will is. (Ephesians 5:15–17)

Understanding the Lord's will comes as we are transformed by His Word. That means that we take the Word and truly bring it into our lives by living out its principles in our daily walk of faith. If we take the following three commands and really strive to live them out in our lives, the Spirit will bring about the needed transformation.

1. Be Filled with the Spirit

> Do not get drunk on wine, which leads to debauchery. Instead, be filled with the Spirit. (Ephesians 5:18)

The practical application: What or who is controlling your life? We are given this wonderful word picture of how wine can take control of people and make them act differently—or we can be controlled by the Holy Spirit and act as the Lord desires us to act. It truly is a choice that we must make. Will we give Him more of ourselves, or will we keep certain areas of our lives under our own control? Simply stated: Will I humbly follow the Spirit's leading, or will I try to keep control of my life?

If you continue reading to the end of Ephesians 5, you will see some of this new life we have available to us. Humbly pursue these character changes, and you will naturally give yourself over to the Spirit's control and will be energized in your walk of faith.

The humility in the husband-wife relationship that

we see in Ephesians 5 is an excellent example for us to follow. We see how an ordinary human relationship, immersed in humility, can become extraordinary. When we follow God's Word, the Holy Spirit can fill our lives and control us. Then we can impact all our relationships for the Lord.

2. Pray in the Spirit

> Pray in the Spirit on all occasions with all kinds
> of prayers and requests. (Ephesians 6:18)

The practical application: When you pray, do you simply share what's on your heart and mind, or do you also seek the Spirit's leading for His guidance regarding what to talk to God about? There is nothing wrong with sharing our hearts with God, but in addition to this, we need to humble ourselves and seek His guidance in our praying. We are to do everything in light of God's Word, which the Holy Spirit authored through human beings (2 Peter 1:21). The better we know the Word, the more clearly we can understand the Holy Spirit's ministry in our lives. This will help us to better listen to His leading and to know what to ask for from our Father.

One of the most valuable and instructive passages in the Word of God is found in the 176 verses of Psalm 119. There are twenty-two groups of eight verses. Take just three groups of eight verses a day. Spend some time in them, and in just over a week you will see how to better pray in the Spirit. In fact, let me encourage you to spend ample time in all 150 psalms, and I am certain you will more naturally see His guidance for praying in the Spirit.

I've told you what to do, now let me show you how to do it. Let's say you have a friend that has contracted the Corona Virus. The first thing you ask for is that God will heal them. Nothing wrong with this, but very possibly God also wants to accomplish something else, very special in their life, as they go through this sickness. This is where praying in the Spirit comes in.

Look at verses 65-72 of Psalm 119 and you'll see the following areas you can pray for your friend that has the virus: Lord teach him/her: knowledge/good judgment, ongoing obedience to your Word, your decrees, to keep your precepts with all their heart, that they will delight in your Word, and that your Word will become more precious to them than silver and gold.

We must remember that God wants to use everything that happens to us to draw us closer to Himself, so we can become more like our Lord. This will help us develop more and more of the mind of Chirst.

3. Walk in the Spirit

> So I say, walk by the Spirit, and you will not gratify the desires of the flesh. (Galatians 5:16)

The practical application: Our lives are supposed to be different because we have new life in Christ (2 Corinthians 5:17). As you proceed through the rest of Galatians 5, you will discover that walking in the Spirit is done by utilizing the fruit of the Spirit. This is why Paul charges us to put off the old self and put on the new. But this is not just a passing exercise, as you can see in Colossians 3:9–10:

> Do not lie to each other, since you have taken off your old self with its practices and have put on the new self, which is being renewed in knowledge in the image of its Creator.

Paul is trying to show us that our new relationship in Christ should impact every aspect of our daily walk of faith. This not only enriches our spiritual relationships, but it causes the unbelieving world, as they observe us (believers) daily interacting with each other, to see that we are truly different than they are.

Since the day we were saved, the Spirit has been waiting patiently for our surrender and willingness to let Him take the lead in our lives. One of the finest ways to enhance your walk in the Spirit is to follow Paul's charge in Colossians 3. Take the time to study this chapter and to put it into practice. It is essential that we understand the words "set your minds on things above" in verse 2. This means to be mentally disposed toward something. It takes an ongoing, complete commitment to make these changes. It is not just a one-time effort, but it is a way of life.

At the time I am writing this, the Sunday school class I am in is beginning a study in the book of James. Consider the first verse of this delightfully practical book, and discover the most insightful truth about who and what we are now that we are Christians:

> This letter is from James, a slave of God and of the Lord Jesus Christ. I am writing to the "twelve tribes"—Jewish believers scattered abroad. Greetings! (James 1:1 NLT)

As Pastor Bruce is teaching us here at Jasper Bible Church, individual words are important. In our above text, James, the "slave," is Jesus's half-brother. James gave his credentials. Think about this: of all the things he could have said about his relationship with his half-brother, Jesus, the one he grew up with—he refers to himself as a "slave," or "bond servant."

As I mentioned before, a bond servant is one who is a servant—and one who has no rights. James was saved by grace, just as you and I have been saved, and he knew his place within the body of Christ. My question for us is: Do we know our place in the body of Christ?

This is what makes the book of James so practical, yet so dynamic, in regard to our walk of faith. James knew his high calling, but he never ceased to walk in the newness of his position in Christ. Please take this great insight to heart and humbly interact with the Holy Spirit, so He can accomplish all that He, the Father, and the Son desire to accomplish in and through you.

Once we are saved, the faith road ahead of us is wide open to the greatest personal experiences. It is up to us to make use of all that has been given to us. The greatest gift of all, next to our new relationship with the Father and Christ, is our relationship with the Holy Spirit.

Make sure you are getting to personally know Him

better and letting Him take the lead! Look at Paul's charge to the church at Corinth:

> Now it is God who makes both us and you stand firm in Christ. He anointed us, set his seal of ownership on us, and put his Spirit in our hearts as a deposit, guaranteeing what is to come. (2 Corinthians 1:21–22)

He is there for us, and we must fully recognize His presence and His desire to work in and through us.

Closing Challenge

Some of you may wonder why I haven't spent time looking at the fruit of the Spirit:

> But the fruit of the Spirit is love, joy, peace, forbearance, kindness, goodness, faithfulness, gentleness and self-control. Against such things there is no law. Those who belong to Christ Jesus have crucified the flesh with its passions and desires. Since we live by the Spirit, let us keep in step with the Spirit. Let us not become conceited, provoking and envying each other. (Galatians 5:22–26)

Our challenge is to walk in the Spirit so that He can totally change our lives. It is our responsibility to put off the old self, grow spiritually, and become more like our Lord. As you look at Jesus's life, look for these nine qualities of the fruit of the Spirit in His character. We are

not to strive for these qualities, but they grow in us as we become more like Him and as we walk in the Spirit. With all this in mind, look into the spiritual mirror of the Bible; look for the new you. If you love the Word and follow the Spirit's teaching and leading, you will see the fruit in varying degrees developing in your life.

As you live these out in today's world, your restraining influence upon iniquity (the Holy Spirit working through your life) will be clearly seen by others, especially young believers. It will be impossible for the lost not to see your penetrating, spiritual light in the darkness around them.

Please pray to grow in your relationship with the Holy Spirit. Let Him become to you all that the Father and Jesus sent Him to be. We are in this fallen world at this time in history to be used of the Lord to:

- Be the light of the world
- Restrain iniquity
- Be ambassadors for Christ
- Be an influential part of the body of Christ
- Be pleasing to our heavenly Father
- Become more like Jesus

As we have seen, the Holy Spirit is the third person of the Godhead, and He has been sent by the Father to inspire us to become more like Christ as we go through the daily struggles of life. In doing this, we will impact the world for eternity.

Prayer of Thanksgiving and Direction

> *Thank You, Father.* You have given us everything we need to be victorious and to be able to stand boldly for our Lord. Please help us to take to heart the principles from Your truth that will make us more like Your Son. Amen.

Dear reader: I sincerely pray you will take what you have seen throughout the pages of this book and think about it—until you appreciate that all of this is for you. Humble yourself under the mighty influence of the Holy Spirit, as you grow in a biblical relationship with Him. As you let Him lead, may you be captivated as you are utilized to change this world and directly impact others for eternity.

May the Lord bless you.

Your Brother in Christ,

Ron

Order Information

To order additional copies of this book, please visit
www.redemption-press.com.
Also available on Amazon.com and BarnesandNoble.com
or by calling toll-free 1-844-2REDEEM.